PLAYING WITH FIRE
Weapons Proliferation, Political Violence, and Human Rights in Kenya

GW00546533

Human Rights Watch
New York · Washington · London · Brussels

ISBN: 1-56432-275-0
Library of Congress Catalog Card Number: 2002105612

Cover photo: Families displaced by politically motivated violence in the Coast Province of Kenya in mid-1997. © 1997 Reuters Ltd.

Cover design by Rafael Jiménez

Addresses for Human Rights Watch
350 Fifth Avenue, 34th Floor, New York, NY 10118-3299
Tel: (212) 290-4700, Fax: (212) 736-1300, E-mail: hrwnyc@hrw.org

1630 Connecticut Avenue, N.W., Suite 500, Washington, DC 20009
Tel: (202) 612-4321, Fax: (202) 612-4333, E-mail: hrwdc@hrw.org

33 Islington High Street, N1 9LH London, UK
Tel: (171) 713-1995, Fax: (171) 713-1800, E-mail: hrwatchuk@gn.apc.org

15 Rue Van Campenhout, 1000 Brussels, Belgium
Tel: (2) 732-2009, Fax: (2) 732-0471, E-mail: hrwatcheu@skynet.be

Web Site Address: http://www.hrw.org

Listserv address: To subscribe to the Human Rights Watch news e-mail list, send a blank e-mail message to subscribe@igc.topica.com.

Human Rights Watch is dedicated to
protecting the human rights of people around the world.

We stand with victims and activists to prevent
discrimination, to uphold political freedom, to protect people from inhumane
conduct in wartime, and to bring offenders to justice.

We investigate and expose
human rights violations and hold abusers accountable.

We challenge governments and those who hold power to end abusive practices
and respect international human rights law.

We enlist the public and the international
community to support the cause of human rights for all.

HUMAN RIGHTS WATCH

Human Rights Watch conducts regular, systematic investigations of human rights abuses in some seventy countries around the world. Our reputation for timely, reliable disclosures has made us an essential source of information for those concerned with human rights. We address the human rights practices of governments of all political stripes, of all geopolitical alignments, and of all ethnic and religious persuasions. Human Rights Watch defends freedom of thought and expression, due process and equal protection of the law, and a vigorous civil society; we document and denounce murders, disappearances, torture, arbitrary imprisonment, discrimination, and other abuses of internationally recognized human rights. Our goal is to hold governments accountable if they transgress the rights of their people.

Human Rights Watch began in 1978 with the founding of its Europe and Central Asia division (then known as Helsinki Watch). Today, it also includes divisions covering Africa, the Americas, Asia, and the Middle East. In addition, it includes three thematic divisions on arms, children's rights, and women's rights. It maintains offices in New York, Washington, Los Angeles, London, Brussels, Moscow, Dushanbe, and Bangkok. Human Rights Watch is an independent, nongovernmental organization, supported by contributions from private individuals and foundations worldwide. It accepts no government funds, directly or indirectly.

The staff includes Kenneth Roth, executive director; Michele Alexander, development director; Reed Brody, advocacy director; Carroll Bogert, communications director; John T. Green, operations director; Barbara Guglielmo, finance director; Lotte Leicht, Brussels office director; Michael McClintock, deputy program director; Patrick Minges, publications director; Maria Pignataro Nielsen, human resources director; Malcolm Smart, program director; Wilder Tayler, legal and policy director; and Joanna Weschler, United Nations representative. Jonathan Fanton is the chair of the board. Robert L. Bernstein is the founding chair.

The regional directors of Human Rights Watch are Peter Takirambudde, Africa; José Miguel Vivanco, America; Sidney Jones, Asia; Elizabeth Andersen, Europe and Central Asia; and Hanny Megally, Middle East and North Africa. The thematic division directors are Joost R. Hiltermann, arms; Lois Whitman, children's rights; and LaShawn R. Jefferson, women's rights.

The members of the board of directors are Jonathan Fanton, chair; Robert L. Bernstein, founding chair; Lisa Anderson, David M. Brown, William Carmichael, Dorothy Cullman, Gina Despres, Irene Diamond, Fiona Druckenmiller, Edith Everett, Michael Gellert, Vartan Gregorian, Alice H. Henkin, James F. Hoge, Jr., Stephen L. Kass, Marina Pinto Kaufman, Wendy Keys, Bruce J. Klatsky, Joanne Leedom-Ackerman, Josh Mailman, Joel Motley, Samuel K. Murumba, Jane Olson, Peter Osnos, Kathleen Peratis, Catherine Powell, Bruce Rabb, Sigrid Rausing, Orville Schell, Sid Sheinberg, Gary G. Sick, Domna Stanton, John J. Studzinski, Maureen White, Maya Wiley. Emeritus Board: Roland Algrant, Adrian DeWind, and Malcolm Smith.

ACKNOWLEDGMENTS

This report is the result of a field investigation in Kenya carried out over a six-and-a-half week period in April and May 1999, as well as subsequent research conducted primarily from the United States. The investigation in Kenya was carried out by Lisa Misol, researcher with the Arms Division of Human Rights Watch, assisted by Binaifer Nowrojee, senior researcher with the Africa Division of Human Rights Watch, Joost Hiltermann, executive director of the Arms Division of Human Rights Watch, and Ernst Jan Hogendoorn, then a researcher with the Arms Division. Misol conducted further research with support from Monique Ramgoolie and Jessica Olsen, research consultants with the Arms Division, Charli Wyatt, associate with the Arms Division, and Sharda Sekaran, former associate with the Arms Division. The report was written by Misol, with contributions by Hogendoorn and Nowrojee, and was edited by Nowrojee and Hiltermann. It was reviewed by Michael McClintock, deputy program director at Human Rights Watch, and James Ross, senior legal advisor at Human Rights Watch. Production assistance was provided by Charli Wyatt, Patrick Minges, publications director at Human Rights Watch, Veronica Matushaj, photo editor at Human Rights Watch, and Fitzroy Hepkins, mail manager at Human Rights Watch.

We would like to thank the many individuals and organizations who helped make this research possible. We are especially grateful to all the interviewees who told us their story, some of whom took great risks to speak to us, as well as to those who provided invaluable assistance with our field investigation in Kenya. Concerns for their personal safety do not permit us to name them here. In addition, a number of individuals and organizations in Kenya and elsewhere generously shared information and insights. We very much appreciate their contributions, which are cited in the report. We wish to offer special thanks to individuals in the following Kenya-based organizations, as well as the organizations themselves: Africa Peace Forum; Commission for Human Rights and Justice; Kenya Human Rights Commission; Muslims for Human Rights; and Security Research Information Centre. We are particularly indebted to colleagues from the Kenya Human Rights Commission and Muslims for Human Rights. They, like the others we have thanked here, bear no responsibility for the report.

The Arms Division gratefully acknowledges the generous support of the John D. And Catherine T. MacArthur Foundation, the Compton Foundation, and members of the Arms Division Advisory Committee. Human Rights Watch takes sole responsibility for the content of this report.

The report is dedicated to the memory of human rights monitor Joseph Lumumba Obeto.

Table of Contents

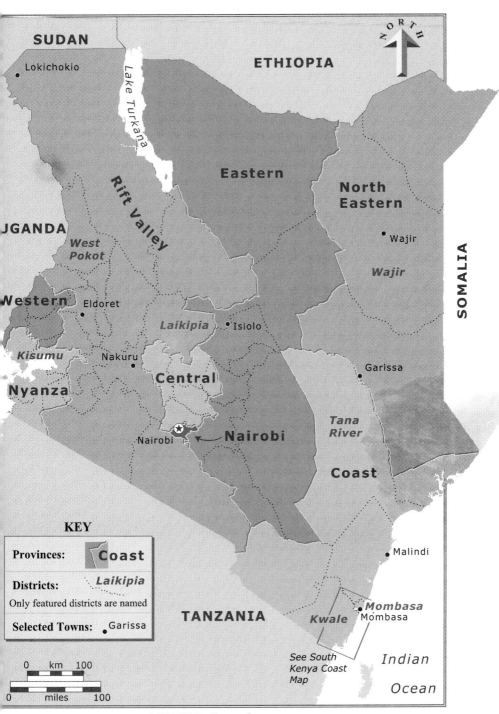

KENYA Provinces

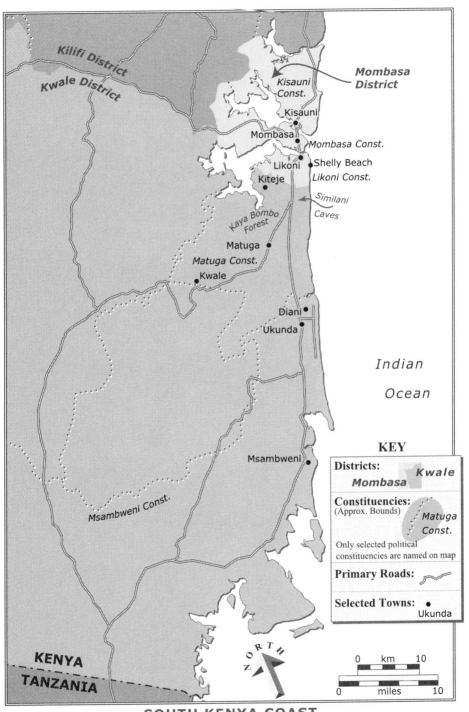

SOUTH KENYA COAST

I. EXECUTIVE SUMMARY

Viewed in contrast to many of its neighbors, Kenya is often seen as a bastion of stability. The country has several strengths that mitigate against the outbreak of mass violence, but it also exhibits many of the factors that have been markers of civil strife elsewhere in Africa: strong ethnic divisions, polarized political issues, political manipulation, rampant violence, socio-economic disparities and a lack of economic opportunity, and endemic corruption. When combined with the increased availability of firearms, this dangerous mix becomes all the more volatile. The easy availability of such weapons within the country contributes to the growing culture of violence that is taking root inside Kenya. In addition to rising crime and generalized insecurity in recent years, the country has experienced repeated flashes of politically inspired ethnic violence, especially during election periods. Those instigating this deadly violence have not been held to account. This continuing pattern of violence and impunity, together with the spread of small arms, threatens Kenyan society and greatly endangers human rights.

Small Arms Proliferation in Kenya

Small arms proliferation across the globe leads to the more rapid spread of violence and magnifies the devastating effects of violence, contributing significantly in areas of armed conflict to human rights abuses and violations of international humanitarian law. In countries emerging from war, the widespread availability of guns contributes to high levels of crime and makes more difficult the transition to a lasting peace. In Kenya and other countries not at war, the ready availability of these weapons undermines security (including with relation to crime), erodes prospects for development, contributes to social disintegration, and makes the resort to violence more likely—and more deadly.

Kenya is vulnerable to weapons trafficking because of its geographic location in a conflict-ridden region. The weapons circulating in Kenya originate from places as far away as China and the United States, but most of them passed through war zones in neighboring countries before making their way to Kenya's illegal gun markets. For years Kenya's territory has been a conduit for weapons shipments destined to nearby areas of violent conflict, but more recently the spread of weapons has spilled back into Kenya itself.

For the time being, guns in Kenya are circulating on a small scale when compared to its war-torn neighbors. They are smuggled into the country a few at a time in a steady flow and sold by traders in secret markets, with some larger-scale illegal arms trafficking also reportedly taking place. The impact of even relatively modest quantities of such weapons, however, is already being felt.

1

The increasing availability of weapons in Kenya has helped fuel rising insecurity and, in some areas, the growing militarization of society. Much media attention has focused on the prevalent use of sophisticated weapons in urban crime, particularly in Nairobi. Often, refugees living in Kenya are scapegoated as the source of these weapons. The proliferation of small arms is most serious along Kenya's northern and western borders, where pastoralist communities have ready access to AK-47s and other automatic rifles obtained from neighboring countries. The introduction and spread of such sophisticated weapons among these communities has intensified conflict and blurred the line between long-standing ethnic competition—traditionally manifested in cattle theft or rustling—and political violence. Guns are now widely used to carry out acts of banditry and cattle rustling in Kenya, and have been responsible for growing numbers of human casualties, including during armed confrontations that pit ethnic groups against each other. This grave insecurity, as rightly noted by a Kenyan civic leader, derives both from "the influx of small arms" and "careless utterances and incitement" by politicians.

Equally disturbing is Kenya's ruling party's use of violence to retain political power since the government was forced to concede to a multiparty system in 1992. It has been estimated that in the past decade at least some 2,000 people have been killed and 400,000 have been displaced in politically motivated violence directed at ethnic groups perceived to support the opposition. High-ranking ruling party officials have been directly implicated in instigating past episodes of violence, and the government has not taken adequate steps to punish the perpetrators. Whereas in the large-scale violence in the early 1990s attackers relied overwhelmingly on traditional weapons such as bows and arrows, attacks in more recent incidents in 1997 and 1998 were carried out with the aid of firearms. Attackers armed with guns enabled others—armed with clubs, machetes, and other crude weapons—to kill, maim, burn, and loot with impunity.

The increased presence of modern weapons facilitates the ability of opportunists in the Kenyan political arena to instigate armed violence for political gain. Similarly, the spread of sophisticated weapons makes it easier for groups under attack to arm themselves in what they portray as self-defense. For the past decade Kenyan political discourse has often embraced the language of violence. Looking to the future, ready access to sophisticated weapons only increases the risk of bloodshed.

Violence for Political Ends: The Coast

This report examines in detail the outbreak of political violence on the Kenyan coast in mid-1997 as a case study of both the orchestration of violence as a political tool and the devastating impact of small arms on human rights. At that time, the country was gearing up for elections and calls for constitutional reform were increasing, putting the ruling party on the defensive. Against this political backdrop, well-organized and well-armed irregular paramilitary forces—known as "raiders"—carried out a series of brash and deadly attacks on non-indigenous residents around Mombasa, Coast Province.

Although the events chronicled in this case study took place several years ago, Human Rights Watch believes that the information is still important, both to document the role of ruling party officials in the violence and to expose the manner in which it was organized, particularly as Kenyans prepare to go to the polls again in general elections that must by law be held in 2002.

The Coast[1] raiders targeted members of ethnic communities that had voted disproportionately against the ruling Kenya African National Union (KANU) party in the 1992 election, causing KANU to lose two of four parliamentary seats in one district that year. As a result of the 1997 attacks these likely opposition voters were forced to flee their homes and, in spite of an unexpected backlash against the government over police abuses, KANU won three of the parliamentary seats in elections later that year, with a fourth seat (the one in the area where the violence was sparked) being won by a KANU ally registered under a new party. In a neighboring district that was also at the center of the violence, KANU won all three parliamentary seats, as it had in 1992. President Daniel arap Moi, who needed to win at least 25 percent of the presidential vote in Coast Province to ensure his reelection, carried the province easily, and his vote tally rose considerably in violence-affected areas that previously had been opposition strongholds.

The perpetrators of the Coast attacks were largely disgruntled local young men whose hostility toward non-indigenous residents of the region led them to support a divisive ethnic agenda that also served the ruling party's political aspirations. Many strongly felt that long-term migrants from other parts of Kenya, as well as other ethnic minority communities settled there, were to blame for the poor conditions faced by their indigenous ethnic group, the Digo. They were motivated by anger over the economic marginalization of the local population, which contrasted sharply with the wealth generated by the area's tourism economy. Their goal was to drive away members of the ethnic groups originating from inland Kenya—the "up-country" population—in order to gain access to jobs, land, and educational opportunities. They used brutal tactics to terrorize their targets for weeks on end.

---

[1] In this report, the term "the Coast" refers to a geographic region known by that name in Kenya, rather than only to areas near the Kenyan coastline.

In a meeting of these interests, a number of local-level KANU politicians and supporters mobilized marginalized Digo youth to take up arms against opposition supporters for political ends. In interviews with Human Rights Watch, several members of the Digo raider force described how the assaults were organized with help from local figures who were politically active with the ruling party. For example, a number of local KANU politicians and supporters were instrumental in recruiting young men to join the raiders. A politically connected spiritual leader used a local cultural practice, oathing, to bind the raiders to secrecy (while promising to make them immune to bullets). He also helped dictate the raiders' targets and strategy. Most of the raiders' commanders had prior military experience, and raiders said some of the rank-and-file members also had previously served in the Kenyan armed services and a few were active-duty servicemen. In addition, the raiders benefited from the participation of a mysterious group of highly trained and well-armed fighters whom they described as soldiers and, in part because they apparently did not speak Swahili, believed were foreigners. The security forces dispatched to quell the violence and subdue the raiders complained that the raiders were very well organized and in many cases better armed and more numerous than they were.

The evidence strongly suggests that higher-level government officials and politicians, acting behind the scenes, also contributed to the organization of the raider force and supported the operations of the raiders once the violence was unleashed. Raiders described several visitors to their training camps, whom they were told were KANU members of parliament (MPs) and key party activists. These visitors met with the raiders' commanders and, according to one raider, sometimes brought food, money, and even guns, as the raiders prepared for action. Other raiders, who were based at different sites or joined later, stated that they only learned of the involvement of national-level political figures after the violence was sparked. They said that these politicians visited their leaders and provided crucial logistical, financial, and political backing during ongoing raids on targeted communities. According to their testimonies, the raiders benefited from both direct and indirect support from the politicians, the latter often supplied via their spiritual leader. In light of the sustained support they received from ruling party politicians, some of the raiders interpreted calls to halt the violence as a sign that it had gone on too long and had become a liability, not as an indicator that the politicians objected to their actions.

Looking back on the events that occurred in 1997, those raiders who decided to speak to Human Rights Watch did so because they felt betrayed and manipulated by the ruling party officials who used and then discarded them. At the time, their aims overlapped with the desire of KANU to purge the area of likely opposition supporters. The raiders' own principal aim was to regain their ancestral land, while ruling party politicians supported them with a view to retaining and winning electoral seats. The raiders now believe their spiritual leader maintained close contact with some of the ruling party's most prominent Coast Province politicians and acted as their local proxy. (KANU MPs later secured the spiritual leader's release from prison after his arrest in August 1997 and funneled large sums of money to him from party funds, lending credence to this claim.) On this basis, the raiders we interviewed maintain that top Coast Province political leaders orchestrated the events from behind the scenes on behalf of the government of President Moi. This interpretation also accords with the testimonies of two former KANU politicians who stated they have insider knowledge that a plot to spark violence in the Coast region was devised at very high levels and involved the Office of the President. (One of those politicians later denied making the statement.)

From the moment the violence erupted until the date of the 1997 general election, the actions of prominent KANU politicians with respect to the raiders were calculated to ensure a victory at the polls. There were several overlapping phases to the politicians' strategy vis-a-vis the ethnic violence. In the beginning, and most violent, stage of the violence, top ruling party politicians in Coast Province acted to support the raiders. Evidence of their support of the raiders' cause included their pressure for the release of the raiders' spiritual leader, visits some politicians made to the raiders' hidden bases, funding (often supplied indirectly, via the raiders' spiritual leader), their public promotion of ethnic federalism—or *majimbo*—and their support for an amnesty for the raiders, offered on the condition that the stolen weapons be returned. In a second phase, KANU politicians encouraged the raiders to rein in the continued violence after early attacks had forced much of the targeted up-country population in the Coast region to flee. The raiders described various attempts to demobilize them as the campaign wound down, by offering jobs and other incentives. In the third phase, after indiscriminate police abuses against the Digo presented a political risk to the party, KANU politicians made explicit attempts to minimize political fallout and bolster the party's support, most notably by enlisting the raiders' spiritual leader to campaign for KANU.

Thus, beyond the action of low-level KANU figures who were intimately involved in the organization of the violence, prominent KANU figures also played a dark role. Having supported the actions of the raiders at an early stage, later efforts to conceal its nature did little to dispel the perception that the ruling party and the Moi government was behind the violence. That measures to rein in the raiders came late and were at best half-hearted compounded this impression.

Despite numerous advance warnings, the government took no action to stop the raiders at an early stage. Once the raids had begun, government security forces did not mount serious security operations and instead took a number of steps that undermined the effective pursuit of the raiders. In addition, they denied effective protection to the victims of the targeted raids and were responsible for a number of serious human rights abuses, including arbitrary arrests and torture, in a crackdown directed in part against opposition party activists whom they accused of being raiders. Moreover, powerful Coast Province leaders intervened to attempt to halt the initial operations of the Kenyan security forces, as well as to stop police investigations and secure the release of arrested politicians. Police investigations were seriously inadequate, leading courts to eventually acquit all but a tiny handful of the accused raiders. In the end, despite hundreds of arrests and a long government inquiry, no one has been brought to justice for organizing the attacks.

Echoes of Rwanda

The state-organized violence in Rwanda before and during the 1994 genocide provides an extreme example of the deadly effect of joining firearms to ethnically driven political violence. The Hutu elite governing Rwanda, determined to hold on to power, deliberately stoked fear and hatred of the Tutsi minority. Beginning in 1990 it directed massacres of Tutsi—and Hutu members of the political opposition—often using militia linked to the ruling party and formed and trained to kill. Once the genocide was launched in April 1994, the authorities continued using the militia and also mobilized citizens in a program of "civilian self-defense" led by soldiers, former soldiers, and police. All the while the Rwandan government described the killings as spontaneous outbursts of ethnic hatred and made no effort to halt the slaughter—much less bring the guilty to justice.

In the months before as well as during the genocide, the government distributed firearms to its civilian supporters. By doing so, it gave them not just the means to kill but also the assurance of having greater power than the unarmed Tutsi, thus making it easier for them to kill without fear. Large massacres—in which thousands of Tutsi were slain—began with attacks by military troops or civilians armed with firearms. The initial slaughter killed a large number of the intended victims, overcame resistance, and paralyzed others with fear, making it easier for later waves of assailants—armed with machetes, clubs, or other similar weapons—to kill with ease.

The perpetrators of the 1997 violence in Kenya's Coast Province employed similar tactics, albeit on a much smaller scale. As in pre-1994 Rwanda, Coast politicians exploited ethnic divisions to preserve and expand their own power. They blamed a group of perceived outsiders whose ethnic identity was taken as an indicator of their support for the political opposition. Drawing on the reserve of ethnic hatred they fomented, politicians mobilized supporters to carry out acts of targeted violence with complete impunity. They began with political attacks carried out by party youth groups and later created a quasi-military organization of youth motivated and trained to kill the designated "enemy." The killers, in turn, depended on guidance from their political leaders, as well as the expertise of highly trained and well-armed military leaders. Their ability to target and wipe out their victims was greatly increased by the use—even the mere possession—of firearms.

In essence, the strategy of the Coast killings, as well as the Rwanda slaughter, hinged on two factors: the manipulation of ethnic divisions into ethnic hatred for political ends and the organization and arming of groups of supporters who could execute or orchestrate widespread killings.

A Time of Transition
With the next national election anticipated for late 2002, the new political landscape in Kenya is one of transition and uncertainty. President Moi, whom the constitution bars from running again, has indicated that he will step down. He arranged to merge KANU with another party and recruited politicians from ethnic groups allied to the opposition, thereby bolstering prospects for his party's electoral success. Moi himself was elected chair of the merged party, a position from which he was anticipated to exercise considerable power. At this writing there was much speculation about whom Moi may intend to be his successor as president, as well as jockeying for position among the contenders for power, but it remained unclear who would emerge as the ruling party's presidential candidate. The opposition had not unified behind a single presidential candidate. In February 2002 five opposition parties announced they would coordinate electoral efforts and, if elected, would share power.

In early 2002, the country also remained focused on the constitutional reform debate. One of the central reform issues under consideration was the devolution of state power. A number of proposals, including a draft put forward by the ruling party in 2001, envision a federalist system. In this context, the term "majimbo" (literally meaning "federalism") again gained currency in the national political debate. The proposals put forward were vague and left the modalities undefined, but politicians who promoted their proposals as pro-majimbo were generally careful to state that they did not wish to promote an ethnically exclusive form of federalism, as had been advanced during previous election campaigns and had served as the rallying-cry for past incidents of politically motivated ethnic violence.

Nevertheless, some Kenyans, mindful of past violence carried out in the name of majimbo, remained wary.

Events in 2001 and early 2002 showed that violence continued to mar Kenyan politics. For example, parliamentary by-elections in early 2001 were associated with serious violence. Violence against opposition activists continued, with police cracking down on government critics in numerous incidents, and pro-KANU youth gangs attacking political opposition rallies. Sporadic violence between members of ethnic groups seen to be allied to the ruling party and those perceived to support the opposition continued in the run-up to the 2002 election. Inter-ethnic fighting in late 2001 in the interior of Coast Province, as well as episodes of such violence in Nairobi in late 2001 and early 2002, claimed dozens of lives. Many observers considered that politicians were to blame for inflaming existing tensions. In addition, violence between well-armed pastoralist communities in northwest Kenya continued and at times threatened to escalate. Tensions remained high in northern border areas, with both local and cross-border attacks contributing to the insecurity and bloodshed, and arms inflows appeared to continue unabated. With the growing presence of guns, Kenyans expressed increasing concern about the spread of violence. Fearful of the potential for ethnic violence tied to the 2002 electoral campaign, members of communities that had been victims of past attacks told Human Rights Watch in 1999 that they themselves had begun organizing self-defense groups and procuring weapons, and reports to that effect have continued.

The government has recognized some of the grave dangers small arms proliferation poses for the country and is working with regional partners to stem the tide of weapons with a focus on information-sharing, enhanced border controls, and harmonization of legislation. It also has sought international assistance to curb weapons flows. Its efforts are welcome, but its approach and implementation leave much to be desired. As with other security issues, it has cracked down on select targets only. It rightly has recognized the role of external actors, especially arms exporters in Europe and Asia who flood the region with weapons, as well as armed groups in neighboring countries who supply recycled weapons to Kenya. But it has been loath to examine its own practices, including its role as a transit point for regional weapons flows. Instead, it has scapegoated refugee populations for illegal weapons flows within the country, often associating all refugees indiscriminately with the actions of armed and criminal elements. International donors, concerned with the potential for terrorist attacks in the wake of the 1998 bombings in Kenya and Tanzania and, more recently, attacks in the United States in 2001, have not questioned this approach. Most dangerously, the international community to date has disregarded the potentially explosive link between weapons availability and domestic political violence.

A Note on Methodology

Our work is intended to complement previously published accounts by nongovernmental groups that examined, among other topics, the causes of the violence in Coast Province, its impact on civilians and the December 1997 general election, and the role played by politics and individual politicians in the bloodshed. We have focused sharply on one dimension of the violence: its organization. In addition to our own interviews, we have relied heavily on sworn testimonies and cross-examinations offered by government and individual witnesses as part of an eleven-month commission of inquiry into Kenya's so-called ethnic clashes formed in 1998 and known as the Akiwumi Commission, after Justice Akilano Akiwumi, the commission's chair. The report submitted by the Akiwumi Commission to the president in August 1999 has not been made public, and little if any further action has been taken by the government. Our request in 1999 for access to the official statements from the Akiwumi Commission was rejected. This notwithstanding, we have in a number of cases had access to official transcripts of the Akiwumi hearings, provided by a participant in the commission's proceedings, as well as testimonies before the commission that have been reproduced in the press. We have supplemented these accounts of sworn testimonies before the Akiwumi Commission with documents provided by some of the witnesses. We have also reviewed documents and unofficial transcripts of the criminal trials of accused raiders, in this case provided by a lawyer for the defense.

For this report, Human Rights Watch set out to investigate the impact of weapons inflows on the level and nature of political violence in Kenya. To find the answers to some of the sensitive questions we intended to ask, we went directly to those with first-hand knowledge: the perpetrators of the violence, as well as the victims. Gathering testimonies from the perpetrators presented serious investigative challenges, as those with whom we wanted to speak often lived in hiding or in fear. With the assistance of local interlocutors, we identified and interviewed five young men who described in detail their direct participation in violent attacks in Coast Province, as well as one who was recruited to become a raider but said he did not take part in the raids. We also spoke with a number of witnesses or victims of the violence and others who had intimate knowledge of the events in question, sometimes using an interpreter. Whenever possible, we conducted interviews individually and in private. For the most sensitive interviews, we also selected locations where the interviewees would not feel threatened, and did not disclose what other interviewees had told us.

As nearly two years had elapsed since the events described by our primary sources, particular care was required to cross check claims and to assess statements that could have been influenced by either extensive news reports or hazy memories—or were deliberate misinformation. Some of the information these sources provided was incomplete or relied on circumstantial evidence and conjectures, and corroborating their testimonies was difficult. Nevertheless, we found that the former raiders were forthcoming about the extent of their participation in the violence. Nor did most express regret, so we do not think they sought to blame others for the violence in order to avoid full responsibility.

Importantly, their testimonies essentially told a consistent story—a story that had not previously been comprehensively told. It is the story of why and how large groups of highly disaffected youths in pursuit of an ethnically exclusive political agenda were recruited, armed, trained, and led to carry out brutal attacks on civilians from other ethnic groups. It is, tellingly, a microcosm of the politically motivated and militarily organized brutality that, on an immensely larger scale, unleashed a genocide in Rwanda and devastating ethnic violence elsewhere in Africa. Our hope is that it serves as a warning to prevent further bloodshed in Kenya and beyond.

II. KEY RECOMMENDATIONS

Human Rights Watch calls on the Kenyan government to take comprehensive measures to address the problems of firearms availability and organized political violence, as well as the relationship between them. Detailed recommendations can be found in Chapter IX. Our main recommendations to the Kenyan government are:

- Take action to prevent politically motivated violence and ensure accountability for past incidents of such violence, including incidents carried out with state sponsorship. Specifically, make public in full the findings and recommendations of the government's commission of inquiry into ethnic violence (the Akiwumi Commission); impartially investigate all allegations of violence, incitement to violence, and other crimes; bring the perpetrators to justice, regardless of their political affiliation; and renounce violence by the ruling party.

- Ensure accountability of local security structures. Apply strict norms of discipline and accountability to the police reservist program or disband it. Bar the formation of community militias. Do not permit local communities to take on or share in law-enforcement functions without strict oversight, proper training, full adherence to legal standards that are consistent with human rights norms, and accountability.

- Strengthen legal controls. In particular, revise legislation related to firearms and ammunition to ensure that it reflects the highest standard and is comprehensive. This should encompass the manufacture, possession, and transfer of these weapons—inclusive of export, import, sale, transshipment, and transport—both within Kenya and with respect to international transactions. Strictly enforce these legal controls, including by: ensuring that security forces are adequately trained and equipped; enhancing the capacity of customs officials to identify and inspect suspicious cargo; combating corruption among law enforcement personnel; and ensuring accountability for misconduct.

Moreover, we call on Kenya's international donors and the international community to:

- Work with the Kenyan government and other regional actors to enhance security and reform the security sector, to address the demand for weapons and the culture of violence, and to encourage progress with

11

respect to small arms controls, while ensuring that in all cases human rights (including refugee rights) are not compromised.

- Insist on governmental accountability for past incidents of ethnic and political violence involving agents of the state at any level, and press for needed reforms, as specified above, to prevent further such violence.

- Exercise restraint with respect to arms transfers to East Africa and the Great Lakes region, as well as other areas of violent conflict and countries where the diffusion of weapons could generate or contribute to a potentially excessive and destabilizing accumulation of weapons and thereby put human rights in danger.

Part 1: Weapons Inflows and the Impact of Regional Conflict

III. WEAPONS INFLOWS AND THE IMPACT OF REGIONAL CONFLICT

President Moi, in power since 1978, has publicly denounced the impact on Kenya of illegal weapons flows from neighboring countries. At a government conference on the proliferation of small arms hosted by Kenya in March 2000, marking Kenya's official entry into a growing international debate on the issue, Moi noted that the unchecked flow of small arms in the region, among other devastating consequences, "undermines peace, intensifies violence and impacts on crime."[2] The Kenyan government has since been a proponent of international action to better regulate transfers of these weapons. Under a United Nations definition, small arms are hand-held firearms—such as revolvers, self-loading pistols, rifles, submachine-guns, assault rifles, and light machine-guns—designed for use by one person.[3] Light weapons, a closely-related category, are designed for use by several persons serving as a crew.

External Weapons Sources and the Spillover Effect of Regional Conflict

Much of East Africa and the Horn of Africa is flooded with guns, predominantly small arms, and a large number of those weapons spill over into Kenya. Since the late 1970s the countries bordering Kenya to the north (Ethiopia, Somalia, Sudan, and Uganda) have experienced long periods of unrest and internal armed conflict. During the cold war these wars were fueled in part by the huge quantities of arms pumped into East Africa by the United States, the Soviet Union, and their allies. The torrent of free or subsidized arms flowing to the African continent subsided significantly after the end of the cold war, but large quantities of arms have continued to pour into the region from numerous arms producers, including China, Bulgaria, and other countries of central and eastern Europe.[4]

---

[2] "Statement by His Excellency Hon. Daniel T. arap Moi," given at the Great Lakes Region and the Horn of Africa Conference on Proliferation of Small Arms and Light Weapons," Nairobi, Kenya, March 14, 2000, p. 3.

[3] Secretary General to the U.N. General Assembly, "Report of the Panel of Governmental Experts on Small Arms in pursuance of GA resolution 50/70 B," A/52/298, August 27, 1997.

[4] See, for example, Human Rights Watch, "Global Trade, Local Impact: Arms Transfers to all Sides in the Civil War in Sudan," *A Human Rights Watch Report*, vol. 10, no. 4 (A), August 1998; "Bulgaria: Money Talks—Arms Dealing with Human Rights Abusers," *A Human Rights Watch Report*, vol. 11, no. 4 (D), April 1999.

Adding to the flow originating from distant countries, a huge quantity of weapons entered the private arms market with the fall of governments in Ethiopia (1991), Rwanda (1994), Somalia (1991), and Uganda (1979 and 1986), as well as conflicts in other African countries.[5] Some governments in East and Central Africa have amply supplied rebel forces in other countries with guns and ammunition, thereby adding to the number of weapons in circulation.[6] Fighters from wars in these countries are a prime source of weapons brought into Kenya, which they often sell for subsistence. Moreover, a number of East African states are also developing their own arms producing industries. Kenya itself, with Belgian assistance, built a bullet manufacturing plant in Eldoret capable of producing 20 million rounds a year, and such secrecy surrounds the plant that little is known about who purchases those bullets and whether they are available for export. In addition, kinship ties among pastoralist communities that straddle international borders can facilitate the movement of firearms from one side to another, as well as the spread of localized conflicts.

The patterns of weapons movements largely reflect the situation of widespread armed conflict in the region. Somalia has been a prominent source of arms since the early 1990s. Unconfirmed estimates for the volume of arms entering Kenya from Somalia range as high as 5,000 automatic rifles per month, with recovered weapons reportedly showing Chinese, U.S., and Bulgarian markings.[7] As fighting in Somalia has quieted down and armed violence has flared up elsewhere in recent years, weapons siphoned from conflicts in Sudan and Uganda have become increasingly common.

In addition, Kenya has long been a major transit point for weapons shipments destined to war-torn countries in the Great Lakes region of Africa. For example, a large weapons shipment destined to Burundi passed through Kenya's Mombasa port before being impounded by Ugandan authorities in October 1999. A Ugandan official cited concern that new weapons flows would aggravate the war in Burundi

---

[5] For example, when Ugandan dictator Idi Amin was forcibly deposed in 1979, the Moroto Army Barracks were looted and an estimated 15,000 guns and approximately two million rounds of ammunition were stolen by local Karimojong warriors. Curtis Abrahams, "Why Disarming the Karimojong has not been an Easy Choice," *EastAfrican Weekly* (Nairobi), March 17-23, 1997.

[6] See, for example, Human Rights Watch, "Global Trade: Local Impact."

[7] Robert Muggah and Eric Berman, *Humanitarianism Under Threat: The Humanitarian Impacts of Small Arms and Light Weapons*, Special Report No. 1 (Small Arms Survey: Geneva, July 2001), p. 10.

as the reason for postponing delivery. Regional sanctions imposed on Burundi in 1996 barred arms shipments, but those sanctions had been lifted in early 1999.[8]

According to Julius Miyumo, a former top Kenyan customs official familiar with the Burundi shipment and others, no explicit legal criteria exist in Kenya for determining whether an arms shipment should be permitted to transit the country, but in practice national authorities halt weapons shipments if they appear to violate a U.N. or regional arms embargo or if the arms cargo has not been properly declared. The existence of an abusive armed conflict in the recipient country and the risk of the weapons being diverted to an unauthorized third party (or of spilling back into Kenya), however, are not considered. Moreover, he explained that according to existing procedures Kenyan authorities designate sensitive cargo (including weapons shipments) "classified" upon the request of the recipient government, and all classified shipments are exempt from inspection, regardless of their content.[9]

The large quantities of weapons transshipped through Kenya to areas of violent conflict thus add significantly to the stocks of weapons in the region. Given the ease of weapons flows across borders, arms purchases by regional actors that are facilitated by the Kenyan government contribute to the problem in Kenya itself of weapons recycled from war. The Moi government, however, has not acknowledged this link and, to the contrary, has spoken of international arms flows to the region as if Kenya itself were not implicated in the trade. For example, without any apparent irony, President Moi expressed concern about armed conflicts in the Horn of Africa and their wider impact on stability in the region, noting: "In particular, I would like to register Kenya's strong opposition to the shipment of arms to the various theaters of conflicts or any other forms of external interventions in the region as these can only further fuel the conflicts as well as increase the human suffering."[10]

---

[8] "Uganda confiscates large arms shipment on way to Burundi," Associated Press, October 19, 1999; "Uganda releases arms for Burundi," *New Vision* (Uganda), BBC Monitoring, October 31, 2000.

[9] Human Rights Watch interview with Julius B. Miyumo, Head of Tax Programmes and New Business Initiatives, Kenya Revenue Authority, and former deputy customs commissioner, Addis Ababa, Ethiopia, April 25, 2001. Miyumo stated that Kenyan customs officials routinely escort classified cargo to the border and hand it over to the authorities of the importing country.

[10] Judith Achieng, "Conflict-Horn of Africa: Illegal Arms Flow Worries Kenya," Inter Press Service (IPS), February 3, 2000.

Moreover, Kenya is vulnerable to illicit weapons trafficking through the same channels used for legal arms shipments. The Kenyan coastline and in particular Mombasa's port have been identified as entry points used by smugglers. United Nations investigators have reported suspicious arms flights that have transited Nairobi and suggested the weapons on board may have been destined to embargoed parties.[11] Former customs official Miyumo, who also served on a U.N. expert panel on small arms, pointed out that the work of customs officers has been made much more difficult by unscrupulous arms brokers and shipping agents who use false documents, misdeclare cargo, file false flight plans, hide weapons in secret compartments in motor vehicles and shipping containers, and otherwise plot to traffic weapons undetected. He indicated that Kenyan customs authorities take a number of steps to rein in such behavior, but said better techniques and equipment were required to more systematically halt undeclared arms shipments.[12]

In all cases, however, the decision to impound or release an unauthorized shipment, as well as when to authorize an arms shipment through Kenyan territory, ultimately depends on political authorities in Nairobi. Miyumo stated that he was aware of two cases in which undeclared (and presumably unauthorized) weapons cargo detained by customs officials was later claimed by a neighboring country and, on the instruction of officials in Nairobi, the arms were released.[13]

Weapons Movements in Kenya

The vast majority of firearms in private hands throughout the country are illegal. It is difficult to obtain a license to own a gun in Kenya, and the unlawful possession of a gun is punishable with long prison sentences. The sale of firearms by unlicensed dealers is also subject to penalties, although much lighter and less commonly enforced. In general, analysts who conducted research on Kenya's legal controls found that, while there was room to tighten penalties further and close

---

[11] United Nations, *Supplementary report of the Monitoring Mechanism on Sanctions against UNITA,* U.N. Document S/2001/966, October 2001, paras. 86-104.

[12] Human Rights Watch interview with Julius B. Miyumo, Addis Ababa, Ethiopia, April 25, 2001; Julius B. Miyumo, "Role of Customs in Small Arms" and "Kenya Revenue Authority," papers distributed at a conference organized by the Bonn International Center for Conversion (BICC) and co-hosted by the U.N. Economic Commission for Africa (UNECA) and the International Resource Group on Disarmament and Security in the Horn of Africa (IRG), titled "Curbing the Demand Side of Small Arms in IGAD States: Potentials and Pitfalls," Addis Ababa, Ethiopia, April 23-26, 2001 (hereafter the BICC conference on "Curbing the Demand Side...").

[13] Human Rights Watch interview with Julius B. Miyumo, Addis Ababa, Ethiopia, April 25, 2001.

loopholes, the major weakness of the firearms legislation was the poor enforcement of existing provisions.[14]

Illegal gun movements in Kenya happen in secret and are difficult to document. Most of the weapons entering Kenya's illegal market appear to be trickling in, transported by small-time traders. Taken together, they account for a steady arms influx. Kenya's border is porous and in large part arid and thinly populated. Although there are nominal customs checkpoints at the main Kenyan entry points, the rest of the border is rarely patrolled and there are many smuggler's routes. The Kenyan police commissioner conceded this point: "The borders with our neighbors are expansive. Even if you take all the police officers in Kenya (about 35,000) to patrol the borders they cannot prevent the flow of guns. There are so many panya [smuggling] routes."[15] Even main roads can be used for the cross-border transport of illegal guns. According to a gun trader, a small bribe of 200 to 300 Kenyan shillings (Ksh.), approximately U.S.$3 to $4, will ensure that a customs official looks the other way.[16]

Traders find it worthwhile to smuggle guns into Kenya because they command a much higher price there. For example, in 1999 Sudan People's Liberation Army (SPLA) deserters reportedly could sell an assault rifle to pastoralist Karimojong traders on the Sudan/Uganda border for 30,000 Ugandan shillings (approximately $20), the Karimojong traders would in turn sell the weapons to Pokot traders living on the Uganda/Kenya border, who could sell it in Kenya for Ksh.10,000 (approximately $135). That same gun could then be sold in Nairobi for as much as Ksh.40,000 (approximately $530). In addition, it is not unusual in Kenya for guns to be bartered for other commodities. On the Kenyan

---

[14] Firearms Act (Laws of Kenya), Chapter 114; Human Rights Watch telephone interview with Kiflemariam Gebrewold, SALIGAD Project Director, BICC, March 30, 2001, drawing on the preliminary results of commissioned research to be published by BICC as Brief No. 23.

[15] "Arms war tough, concedes Abong'o," *Daily Nation* (Nairobi), August 2, 2001.

[16] Human Rights Watch interview with a gun dealer, Nairobi, June 28, 1999.

border guns can be exchanged, depending on the current supply, for two goats or a cow.[17]

Prices fluctuate depending on demand, supply, location, and the type of weapon for sale. In some parts of northern Kenya, prices may run as low as Ksh.5,000 ($65) for a firearm, while ammunition was estimated to cost Ksh.80-100 (U.S. $1 to $1.25) per round. Researchers found that just inside the Kenya-Somali border, where guns are plentiful, an AK-47 assault rifle could be had in late 2000 for Ksh.10,000 ($130), with the price increasing to Ksh.15,000 (almost $200) in Garissa, further inside the border province. The German-designed G3 assault rifle, carried by Kenyan security forces, is more expensive than the AK-47, commanding a price of Ksh.15,000 (nearly $200), but part of the G3's appeal is that ammunition for it is easier to buy. In 2001, during a time of relative shortage, it was reported that AK-47s sold by SPLA fighters to arms merchants in eastern Ugandan commanded a price of $90 to $147 each, a pistol could be purchased for approximately $30, and a rifle could be traded for a bag of sorghum.[18]

There is a thriving market for guns in the border areas, with demand for such weapons fueled by local and cross-border cattle raids, as well as armed border incursions. In addition, many of the weapons that traders smuggle into Kenya are transported to the interior of the country. They are sometimes smuggled by boat, but most often carried aboard commercial vehicles used to transport livestock or other merchandise. One common destination is Lokichokio near the borders with Sudan and Uganda, reputed to be a center of the illegal trade in firearms and ammunition in northwest Kenya.

---

[17] See E. Ogoso Opolot and a special correspondent in Karamoja, "Rising Armed Crime Linked to SPLA Guns," *EastAfrican Weekly*, September 13-20, 1999; Human Rights Watch interview with a gun dealer, Nairobi, June 28, 1999; Rukia Subow, Pastoralist Peace and Development Initiative (PPDI), "The Proliferation of Small Arms and Pastoralists in the Horn of Africa," statement given at the U.N. conference on small arms, July 2001. All monetary figures have been converted to U.S. dollars using the exchange rates that prevailed at the time of the transactions. The conversions were performed using an online currency converter available at http://www.oanda.com/converter/fxhistory (March 28, 2002).

[18] See Lt. Col. H.I. Hussein, acting head of security, Kenyan Armed Forces, "The Effects of Small Arms Proliferation on Banditry and Rustling in Northern Kenya: A Military Perspective," presentation made at the BICC conference on "Curbing the Demand Side...," p. 2; Ebla Haji Aden, PPDI, "Small Arms Proliferation in Garissa District: Reasons Behind the Demand and Supply," paper presented at the BICC conference on "Curbing the Demand Side...," pp. 2-3; "Uganda/Sudan: Guns for $30 in the Border Markets," *Indian Ocean Newsletter*, March 17, 2001.

Isiolo, gateway to Kenya's vast arid north (and on the Transafrica highway), is also reputed to be a hub for arms trafficking. In 1997, for example, Kenyan police closed a market near Isiolo that was known as an "arms supermarket," but the illegal trade continued in a more discreet fashion.[19] One person described to Human Rights Watch traveling the same year to a clandestine open-air gun market outside Isiolo to purchase an AK-47 assault rifle.[20] There, he said, dozens of guns were available for sale, transported by arms dealers who packed the weapons, disassembled, inside hidden chambers in the backs of their four-wheel drive vehicles. The informal and illegal market, according to him, moved from place to place in the Isiolo area to avoid detection.

Much of the country's gun trade happens on an even smaller scale. Kenya's thriving illegal arms market is largely supplied by impoverished rebels, well-armed herders, and corrupt members of the security forces. Acting individually, they sell their equipment to small-scale arms dealers who in turn illegally supply the market. In one example, after a month-long investigation of an "arms syndicate" that led to the arrest of four suspects, police recovered two assault rifles and less than one hundred rounds of ammunition, which reportedly had been obtained from military or police sources.[21] A gun trader who spoke to Human Rights Watch explained that he does not keep a stock of weapons to sell, but rather travels to Isiolo or the Uganda border area to purchase firearms one or a few at a time at the request of clients.[22] He added that although he has been involved in the trade for a number of years he sells weapons from time to time only and otherwise runs a legitimate business. According to him, his case was fairly typical because it is simply too dangerous to keep many weapons on hand to sell.

Larger-volume weapons sales for the private market also reportedly take place in Kenya. According to a top firearms control official, some wealthy individuals are involved in arms smuggling activities in Kenya and supply weapons to criminal networks.[23] Kenya is also home to arms dealers who are involved in brokering weapons shipments for clients in other African countries, and their presence in Kenya has at times fed speculation that these individuals may also arrange to sell on the domestic firearms market. Moreover, an arms-trade researcher who in 2000 investigated Kenya's role as a major transshipment point for arms cargo reported

---

[19] Ken Opala, "Flourishing trade in guns," *Daily Nation*, March 26, 1997.

[20] Human Rights Watch interview with an owner of an illegal gun, Nakuru, Kenya, May 14, 1999.

[21] "Police unearth arms syndicate," *Daily Nation*, August 10, 2000.

[22] Human Rights Watch interview with a gun dealer, Nairobi, June 28, 1999.

[23] "Gunrunning is out of control, admits State," *Daily Nation*, February 14, 2001.

that some of the weapons meant to pass through the country on their way to other destinations in fact were being siphoned off for sale inside Kenya, largely as a result of corrupt practices at transit and border points.[24] She indicated that, in addition to small-scale arms dealing involving corrupt police and individuals, large syndicates were also involved in illegal cross-border arms movements.

Many of the illegal firearms available for purchase can be found in Kenya's urban centers. Certain neighborhoods in Nairobi in particular have earned a reputation as centers of the illicit gun trade. The gun trader with whom Human Rights Watch met was located in Eastleigh, one of the areas often mentioned in connection with illegal gun sales. In another Nairobi neighborhood, a team of journalists went undercover to purchase a handgun and were offered a range of sophisticated weapons. Arms dealers even rent sophisticated weapons, with an AK-47 reportedly available for hire in mid-2001 for $30.[25]

Preliminary findings from an ongoing study of firearms availability in Nairobi indicate that the major staging points for weapons trafficking destined to Nairobi, in addition to Isiolo in central Kenya and Lokichokio near the Uganda border are: Garissa near the Somali border; Mombasa on the coast; Eldoret, Kisumu, and Nakuru in western Kenya; and Wilson airport in Nairobi.[26]

Blaming Refugees

Although weapons circulation in Kenya is complicated and usually involves many actors, the government typically attributes weapons trafficking, along with other crimes, to refugees living in Kenya and indiscriminately accuses refugees of being the major source of insecurity. For example, the senior official responsible for firearms licensing stated: "Many refugees immigrating from neighboring war-torn countries carry with them all manner of firearms" and identified the "majority" of refugees as former fighters who "cross the borders with the weapons and sell them for subsistence."[27]

---

[24] Human Rights Watch telephone interview with Kathi Austin, Fund for Peace Arms and Conflict Program, April 17, 2001; Human Rights Watch email communication with Kathi Austin, March 14, 2002.

[25] "Over 5,000 unlicensed guns in Nairobi," *Daily Nation*, July 12, 1999; Simon Robinson, "Kalashnikovs for Hire," *Time*, July 30, 2001; "Police promise to reward informers on illegal firearms," KBC Radio, FBIS, July 5, 2001.

[26] Kizito Sabala, Africa Peace Forum (APFO), "The Proliferation, Circulation and Use of Illegal Firearms in Urban Centres: The Case of Nairobi, Kenya," presented at the BICC conference on "Curbing the Demand Side...," p. 2. The final paper is to be published by BICC as Brief No. 23.

[27] "Gunrunning is out...," *Daily Nation*.

President Moi himself has argued that refugees are largely to blame for bringing guns and crime into Kenya, and the top official in North Eastern Province has blamed arms trafficking on the refugee community living in camps.[28] More than 200,000 refugees have sought refuge in Kenya from neighboring countries. The frequent xenophobic or anti-refugee statements, police harassment, arbitrary arrests and extortion by government officials have created an increasingly hostile environment for the thousands of refugees not implicated in arms trafficking.

In the name of security, the government has confined most refugees to camps in underdeveloped and insecure areas, one in North Eastern Province close to the Somali border and another in northwestern Rift Valley Province near the Sudan and Uganda borders. For those refugees and asylum-seekers who remain in Nairobi, particularly Somalis, police harassment and roundups are a constant problem. It is often only with bribes that refugees can avoid arbitrary arrest and detention. The activities of the police are periodically intensified, as happened in September 1998, when roundups were carried out in a more widespread fashion, and refugees were asked to surrender their "protection letters" from the United Nations High Commissioner for Refugees (UNHCR) without being given another document in replacement.

The Kenyan government has legitimate security concerns with regard to those who seek to use refugee cover to traffic arms, conduct cross-border military activities, or evade prosecution for criminal acts they have committed previously in their own country or elsewhere. Criminal elements among the refugee population have been identified as being actively involved in arms trafficking, banditry, and other illegal acts in and near the refugee camps, particularly in North Eastern Province. It has been alleged that arms have been introduced into a refugee camp in that province and temporarily stored there.[29] The bulk of refugees in Kenya, however, do not participate in criminal activity and those that do, including those in camps, are subject to criminal proceedings under Kenyan law. Many refugees are themselves victims of armed violence, with residents of the refugee camps being especially vulnerable to attacks and violent crime.

While national and border security issues are clearly a priority for any government, no government can, in the name of security, trample on the rights of

---

[28] Ken Opala, "US keeps eye on Moi exit," *Daily Nation*, April 13, 2001; Victor Obure, "Govt recovers over 200 guns," *East African Standard*, July 27, 2001.

[29] Kathi Austin, "Armed Refugee Camps: A Microcosm of the Link Between Arms Availability and Insecurity," presentation at a workshop organized by the Social Science Research Council's Program on Global Security and Cooperation, titled "Workshop on International Law and Small Arms Proliferation," Washington, DC, February 6, 2002.

refugees. The responsibilities of a government to ensure national security and to uphold its obligation to respect refugee rights are not contradictory. To the contrary, long-term security interests are best served through the implementation of mechanisms that uphold the rule of law. Ultimately, abusing the human rights of refugees and indiscriminately penalizing refugees without due process or individual accountability is neither an acceptable option under international law nor does it provide the most effective and sustainable domestic security policy.

The Kenyan government can take other, more just steps to address security and prevent covert rebel activity, such as increased police patrols and intelligence surveillance along the border or among communities with high numbers of refugees, the relocation of the refugee camps and settlements with refugees further away from the borders with Somalia, Sudan, and Uganda, and the impartial investigation and prosecution of those individuals responsible for criminal activity, be they Kenyans or non-nationals. Each of these proposals is less restrictive than the indefinite confinement of thousands of people who have not historically jeopardized Kenya's safety, and would allow for a more sustainable and rights-respecting security policy over the long-term.

The Domestic Impact

The increasing availability of weapons has helped drive rising insecurity and crime in Kenya, where guns are commonly used to commit a range of violent acts. There are reportedly large numbers of illegal guns in the capital, and high levels of armed crime fuel a high demand for firearms licenses across the country.[30] Underscoring the scale of the problem in the context of a country not at war, an analysis produced by the U.S. State Department in mid-2001 quoted Kenya's country's top firearms licensing officer as stating that "seventy-five percent of the country is awash with illicit arms" and itself declared that arms proliferation in Kenya had reached crisis proportions.[31]

---

[30] "Over 5,000...," *Daily Nation*; "Gunrunning is out...," *Daily Nation*.

[31] U.S. Department of State Bureau of Intelligence and Research and Bureau of Public Affairs, "Arms and Conflict in Africa," fact sheet, July 9, 2001, available at http://usinfo.state.gov/topical/pol/arms/stories/01070921.htm (March 29, 2002). The fact sheet noted that, while in 2000 the Kenyan police was reportedly recovering between 1,800 and 2,000 unlicensed guns per month in Nairobi, in 2001 an estimated 5,000 illegal firearms remained in circulation in the capital, amounting to one illegal weapon for every 560 Nairobi residents—this without including unrecorded sales, which were expected to be considerably higher.

Generalized Insecurity

In northern Kenya, the presence of guns is strongly felt and is having wide-ranging repercussions. In some areas, especially along the borders, guns are so common that they are openly carried. Violent incidents involving firearms appear to be sharply on the rise, and high numbers of casualties have been reported. Acts of banditry, including armed highway attacks, are widely reported in parts of Coast Province and North Eastern Province.

A Kenyan military expert who has studied small arms availability estimated that there are 40,000 firearms illegally held by communities in northern Kenya and that security forces have recovered less than 10 percent of them, leading to serious concerns that "such huge uncontrolled amounts of firearms could pose a significant threat to the stability of the area and undermine national security."[32] For their part, community leaders in northwest Kenya have repeatedly stated that their communities will not give up their weapons without a guarantee of protection from armed attacks by rivals, including attacks launched from neighboring countries.[33]

Automatic weapons have changed the face of cattle rustling (also known as cattle or livestock raiding) in Kenya's northern border regions. Historically, cattle rustling in Kenya has been defined as the practice in some pastoralist communities of using traditional weapons to take livestock from a competing group, typically at night and using minimum force. More recently, such incidents have evolved into large-scale operations involving the theft, including in daylight, of hundreds or sometimes thousands of cattle; the exchange of gunfire; rape and abduction; and, very often, the killing or wounding of people, including of women and children. As a local religious leader commented in February 2000, "Cattle rustling [incidents] in the North Rift and other parts of the country are no longer [like] the traditional ones. These days, heavy weapons are used and the attacks also target humans."[34] As one example among many, it was reported that raiders brandishing assault rifles and submachine-guns in a February 2001 raid killed thirty people and stole 15,000 head of cattle.[35] It has been estimated that cattle raids in the latter half

---

[32] Hussein, "The Effects of Small Arms Proliferation...," p. 2.
[33] See, for example, "Moi gun order will not work, says MP," *Daily Nation*, April 23, 2001.
[34] "Rustling: OAS is urged to intervene," *Daily Nation*, February 9, 2000.
[35] Stephen Muiruri and Waweru Mugo, "Thirty Killed in Raid," *Daily Nation*, February 9, 2001.

of the 1990s accounted for more than 1200 deaths and the theft of over 300,000 livestock.[36]

The introduction of sophisticated firearms has had far-reaching effects on communities, including social disintegration in some cases and the increasing resort to violence to address long-standing conflicts.[37] Some broad trends are also evident. In particular, guns have become an important trade commodity and provide a means for competing groups to assert and expand territorial control and, hence, access to key resources. In addition, cattle rustling has become commercialized. Stolen livestock have been sold, often across international borders, rather than kept in communities. Theft during cattle raids has increasingly involved other types of assets. Non-pastoralist raiders and youths, in addition to herders themselves, have been drawn into cattle rustling. Cross-border raids are common. More generally, the increased use of firearms has blurred the distinction between conflict and crime.[38]

Although banditry is usually viewed as an act of common crime, and cattle rustling is typically considered a traditional cultural practice, this analysis is flawed because both may at times harbor a political dimension. For example, residents of northern Coast Province have claimed that local government officials sponsor groups of bandits, sometimes unleashing them for political purposes.[39] In addition, the harsh security response of government forces to occasional bandit attacks on

---

[36] Human Rights Watch email communication with a Western security analyst, April 1, 2002.

[37] See Karl Vick, "Small Arms' Global Reach Uproots Tribal Tradition," *Washington Post*, July 8, 2001. In one case, a community-based approach introduced to curb small arms misuse, while showing some promise as a crime control measure, introduced serious new problems. Because there was no legal framework defining its scope and its limits, and because government supervision was inadequate, the community used draconian tactics to pursue suspects, leading to a number of deaths and serious human rights abuses. Peter B. Marwa, SALIGAD regional coordinator, "The Sungusungu in Kuria: Vigilantism or an Indigenous Initiative to Curb the Demand for Small Arms and Light Weapons?," paper presented at the BICC conference on "Curbing the Demand Side..."

[38] See, for example, Kennedy Mukutu, *Pastoralism and Conflict in the Horn of Africa* (Saferworld: London, December 2001); Dr. Paul Goldsmith, "Cattle, Khat and Guns: Trade, Conflict, and Security on northern Kenya's Highland-Lowland Interface," paper presented at a conference on Conflict and Conflict Management in the Horn of Africa, May 1997, pp. 24-33.

[39] Muslims for Human Rights (MUHURI), *Banditry and the Politics of Citizenship: The Case of the Galje'el Somali of Tana River,* (Mombasa: Muslims for Human Rights, 1999), especially pp. 29-34.

government personnel politicizes such incidents, particularly as entire ethnic communities have reportedly been targeted for retaliation. In the case of cattle rustling among pastoralist communities, it is often difficult to distinguish between cattle raids motivated by competition over resources (such as cattle, access to grazing land, and water) and those that are at least partly driven by ethnic chauvinism or political motivations. Often the motives overlap. Moreover, it often has been alleged that cattle raiders are hired by businessmen and politicians for commercial purposes unrelated to the rivalries of pastoral communities.[40]

Armed attacks can unleash a vicious cycle of revenge attacks and escalating arms races between rival communities. This cycle is all the more dangerous when tit-for-tat cattle rustling is further charged with political grievances, as has been the case in and around Wajir District, North Eastern Province. The Wajir area has been the site of repeated outbreaks of armed ethnic violence, including large-scale cattle raids with corresponding loss of life. In one particularly bloody incident on October 25, 1998, in which automatic weapons and reportedly grenades were used, well over one hundred members of the Degodia community were killed and an estimated 17,000 camels, cattle, sheep and goats were stolen. The raid, known as the Bagalla massacre, is believed to have been carried by members of the Borana community with support from ethnic kinsmen from the Ethiopian side of the border, and the attack reportedly followed inflammatory speeches by Kenyan politicians.[41]

The Government's Failure to Provide Security

In the face of widespread armed violence and crime, the Kenyan government has failed to provide adequate security. Affected citizens in the hardest-hit areas often suggest that the main obstacle to greater security is a lack of will on the government's part. An additional explanation for poor security is that police-community relations are tense in some areas. Persistent allegations of widespread corruption in the police forces has further eroded public trust.[42]

---

[40] See, for example, "Cartel is funding cattle rustling, say leaders," *Daily Nation*, July 20, 1999.

[41] Emman Omari, "Killings blamed on incitement," *Daily Nation*, May 6, 1999. A 1999 Kenyan government report on the incident put the death toll at 124 people and claimed that Ethiopian rebels may have participated in the attack. "Government confirms presence of Ethiopian Oromo rebels in northeast," KBC radio, BBC Monitoring, June 22, 1999.

[42] See, for example,"Senior officer says police force in a major crisis," *East African Standard*, BBC Monitoring, October 3, 2000; MUHURI, *Banditry and the Politics of Citizenship*.

Kenyan security officials, even if dedicated to their responsibilities, face difficult challenges in carrying out their duties. Notably, they lack the necessary resources, training, equipment, and personnel to monitor security conditions effectively throughout the country. Moreover, the government presence in some parts of the country is extremely limited and poor or non-existent roads further limit access. Criminals, bandits, and cattle raiders often are better-armed than government forces. Low pay, low morale, and low professionalism among police officers deter them from risking their lives in difficult working conditions and encourage corruption and bribery. In mid-1999 the then-police commissioner for Kenya publicly agreed that personnel shortages and lack of funding were severe constraints on police activities, but maintained—contrary to indications—that police forces were sufficiently well-equipped to confront threats to public security, including well-armed cattle rustlers.[43]

The Militarization of Society

Faced with rising insecurity and the sense that the government security forces are unable or unwilling to protect the populace, Kenyans are increasingly taking matters into their own hands. Whereas many communities have long felt they could protect themselves, if needed, with traditional weapons they already own, such as bows and arrows, this is no longer the case in some parts of the country. For example, two assistant ministers from northern Kenya recommended in early 2001 that their ethnic community purchase guns on its own if the government did not agree to provide weapons for protection from cross-border violence. One stated: "It's imperative for all those living on boundaries to be given the latest model of weapon."[44]

In the northern border regions of Kenya, steadily increasing incidents of armed cattle rustling, especially during periods of drought, have led pastoralist communities to conclude that they should acquire modern automatic weapons. In an ethnically charged environment, such moves have precipitated arms races between communities, as noted above. A religious leader in one particularly hard-hit area in northwest Kenya expressed concern about the successive arming of different ethnic communities: "We have seen the influx of arms methodically getting into the hands of the Turkana, the Pokot [...] and now the Marakwet and the Tugen have started acquiring them. What do you expect next?"[45]

---

[43] "Minister accuses govt over banditry,"*Daily Nation,* June 4, 1999.

[44] "Arm Our People, Government Told," *Daily Nation*, January 28, 2001.

[45] Churchill Otieno, "A 'Kosovo' in the bowels of Kenya's Great Rift Valley," *Daily Nation*, November 12, 1999.

Many pastoralist communities have organized private militias. In these cases, guns typically are not the property of individuals, but are owned by a clan or tribe.[46] In 1999 the National Council of Churches of Kenya (NCCK) reported that its research had unearthed evidence of training camps in the North Rift used by such community militias, a claim the government hotly denied could be true.[47] A more recent study carried out in Kenya's North Eastern Province examined the demand for small arms in one district and found that communities acquired arms for several reasons: to protect lives and property, especially livestock; to assert control over scarce natural resources; and to defend themselves against rival groups and carry out revenge attacks.[48] The study also found that the communities resorted to arming themselves because they had lost faith in the government's ability to guarantee basic security.

The same phenomenon occurred elsewhere as well. In the town of Lokichokio, in the North Rift area, security officials have claimed as many as 90 to 95 percent of households are armed, with the guns no longer being used exclusively for self-defense.[49] The provincial commissioner himself declared:

> We believe that in Northeastern Province every family has a gun in good working condition. We also believe that most major clans have clan militia. We believe that each elder, each religious leader, and each political leader knows where the guns are.[50]

Moreover, as noted above, private individuals reportedly hire youths to engage in cattle raiding, suggesting that they too are readily able to organize private armed groups for their own purposes.

In addition to privately organized armed groups, there are community-based forces known as Kenyan Police Reservists. In principle, their role is to protect

---

[46] Human Rights Watch interview with Mohammed Hassan Mumin, Chairman of the Peace and Development Committee, Wajir, April 4, 1999; Hussein, "The Effects of Small Arms...," p. 2.

[47] "Cattle Rustling and Guns Influx in the North Rift," letter from NCCK General Secretary Mutava Musyimi to Hon. Marsden Madoka, Minister of State, September 11, 1999; "Arms claim denied," *Daily Nation*, October 11, 1999.

[48] Aden, PPDI, "Small Arms Proliferation in Garissa District...," p. 2.

[49] Muggah and Berman, *Humanitarianism Under Threat*, pp. 16, 40.

[50] Mike Crawley, "Kenya trade-in: guns for schools," *Christian Science Monitor*, January 2, 2001.

communities where the government security presence is minimal or ineffective, particularly in areas vulnerable to cross-border attacks. However, through this program the Kenyan government has formed, trained, and armed private citizens whose use of government-issued weapons is subject to few functioning accountability measures.[51] Given that Kenyan authorities distribute G3 rifles and ammunition in a highly decentralized manner, controls are uneven at best and the system can be readily abused.[52] In a rare confirmation of problems with the reservist program, a district official in 1999 admitted that guns distributed to reservists had been used in acts of banditry and said the government needed to vet future reservists to avoid mistakenly recruiting criminals.[53] In another example, after a cattle raid in early 2001 in which some thirty people were killed, a police officer blamed police reservists, saying they "sometimes give out their guns to the [cattle] raiders."[54] Others have openly accused police reservists of participating directly in cattle rustling and banditry, among other crimes.[55]

Not surprisingly under the circumstances, the distinction between private militia and police reservists has sometimes blurred. Moreover, the distribution of weapons under the reservist program has appeared to favor certain communities, those most closely aligned with the ruling party. Such selective arming has contributed to the demand for weapons among rival communities and fueled the perception that rival groups who have been issued government weapons enjoy political sponsorship and impunity for armed attacks.[56]

---

[51] One study reported that chiefs were instructed to conduct annual checks on "homeguards" (referring to police reservists), but this proved "virtually impossible," given migration by pastoralists. Muggah and Berman, *Humanitarianism Under Threat*, p. 66.

[52] For example, community elders in one part of the North Rift reportedly are responsible for recruiting police reservists and in another elders reportedly distribute the government-issued guns. John Mbaria, "Sugata: Valley of Death," *EastAfrican Weekly*, October 9, 2000; Benson Wambugu, "Now Pokots reveal their sources of guns," *People* (Nairobi), April 24-30, 1998.

[53] "Government to withdraw guns from police reservists in Turkana District," KBC radio, BBC Monitoring, January 28, 1999.

[54] Muiruri and Mugo, "Thirty Killed in Raid."

[55] See, for example, "Eleven killed in northwest as Pokot tribesmen repulse Turkana raiders," *East African Standard*, BBC Monitoring, April 3, 2000.

[56] This perception is especially prevalent with respect to the Pokot community in northwest Kenya. For a discussion, see below.

Government Efforts to Combat Small Arms Proliferation

In Kenya, as elsewhere, international attention to the problem of small arms proliferation and misuse has been catalyzed by the global campaign to ban antipersonnel landmines, which culminated in the 1997 Convention on the Prohibition of the Use, Stockpiling, Production, and Transfer of Anti-Personnel Mines and On their Destruction (the Mine Ban Treaty). Kenya is not directly affected by the scourge of anti-personnel landmines, but it has a long-standing if limited problem with unexploded ordnance (UXO), some of which date back as far as the First World War. The government of Kenya signed the Mine Ban Treaty on December 5, 1997, ratified it on January 23, 2001, and the treaty entered into force for Kenya on July 1, 2001.[57]

The Kenyan government has since 2000 publicly and prominently recognized the need to stem the proliferation of small arms—the weapons scourge that causes the most devastation in Kenya. Drawing on growing international attention to the spread of small arms and light weapons, particularly in the lead-up to the first-ever U.N. conference on illicit trafficking in such weapons, held in July 2001, Kenya has taken an active role to promote initiatives to stem small arms proliferation at national, sub-regional, and regional levels; to support calls for international action; and to request international assistance for small arms initiatives in poor countries. While not sufficient, these steps do mark real progress in acknowledging the problem and suggest that the government is willing to take some steps to rein it in.

Most notably, Kenya took the initiative to convene in March 2000 a ministerial-level government conference on small arms in the Horn of Africa and the Great Lakes sub-region. The conference resulted in the Nairobi Declaration, in which ten governments pledged to work together to implement a coordinated regional action plan to stem the proliferation of small arms. In particular, they agreed to improve information-sharing and to harmonize national legislation, giving particular attention to legal controls over the possession and transfer of weapons and the need to improve the institutional capacity of law enforcement bodies. They also called for international support to help them implement agreed measures and designated Kenya to coordinate follow-through. The Nairobi Declaration also recognized (in introductory language) many of the dangers posed by small arms proliferation and acknowledged the need for governments to dedicate themselves to addressing the root causes of demand by reducing poverty, enhancing good governance, observing human rights, and promoting democracy.

---

[57] For more information, see International Campaign to Ban Landmines, *Landmine Monitor Report 2001: Toward a Mine-Free World* (Human Rights Watch: New York, August 2001), pp. 83-85.

Consistent with the position of the Kenyan government, it placed great emphasis on the responsibility of external arms suppliers to rein in the illegal arms trade.

After the Nairobi conference, subsequent meetings resulted in the adoption of a regional plan of action and also contributed significantly to the adoption of a common African position on the problem of small arms proliferation, known as the Bamako Declaration, for consideration at the 2001 U.N. conference.[58] While the weak international plan of action adopted by consensus at the U.N. conference was a disappointment to African and European governments that had called for vigorous international action to control small arms flows, they vowed to continue to work to limit the spread of these weapons and alleviate their humanitarian consequences.[59]

Representatives of civil society, which has been a key actor in drawing attention to the issue, have been active participants in the effort to formulate strategies, carry out programs, and encourage implementation of needed government measures.[60] Regional governments, for their part, have worked with the Kenya small arms secretariat to identify priorities and develop a regional implementation plan. At this writing, an important initiative aimed at strengthening and harmonizing legislation governing small arms and light weapons was underway, with the hope that it would lead to the adoption of a regional legal protocol. However, concrete progress on cross-border cooperation to tackle small arms proliferation was hampered by the fact that signatories to the Nairobi

---

[58] This document, reached at the Organization of African Unity summit in Mali in December 2000, noted the deleterious impact of small arms on society, addressed both the illegal and legal trade in these weapons, focused on the coordination of national efforts into a larger action plan, and called for international assistance. As with the Nairobi document, it focused particular attention on the role of outside arms suppliers.

[59] Kenya's representative was among those voicing that sentiment. Statement by Hon. Marsden H. Madoka at the United Nation Conference on Small Arms and Light Weapons in All its Aspects, New York, July 11, 2001.

[60] See, for example, Africa Peace Forum/International Resource Group (APFO/IRG), "Improving Human Security Through the Control and Management of Small Arms," *Tackling small arms in the Great Lakes region and the Horn of Africa: Strengthening the capacity of subregional organizations*, compiled by Andrew McLean, report of a conference co-hosted by APFO/IRG and the East African Cooperation (EAC) in Conjunction with the Norwegian Initiative on Small Arms Transfers (NISAT), March 23-25, 2000, Arusha, Tanzania; Security Research and Information Centre (SRIC, Nairobi), United Nations African Institute for the Prevention of Crime and the Treatment of Offenders (UNAFRI, Kampala), Saferworld (London), and Institute for Security Studies (ISS, Pretoria) (Pretoria: Institute for Security Studies, 2000).

Declaration have been slow to designate national authorities responsible for carrying out commitments. Moreover, governments had not yet agreed to the agenda for action at the ministerial level, many lacked national implementation plans to guide the work, and some have been slow to share information.[61]

At the national level, the picture is also mixed. The Kenyan government has taken a number of steps consistent with the objectives laid out in the Nairobi Declaration, most of them involving law enforcement measures. For example, it has worked to clear border areas of illegal arms, a process that it said had netted more than a thousand illegal arms in North Eastern Province as of early 2001.[62] Kenya also has repeatedly used temporary gun amnesties to encourage citizens to turn in illegal weapons in exchange for a guarantee they will not face prosecution. (These have met with little success, as they do not address the insecurity and other problems underlying the demand for weapons.)[63]   In February 2001, the government announced that it would introduce legislation to increase penalties for firearms-related violations while simultaneously making firearms licenses more difficult to obtain.[64]   The government also launched an anti-crime campaign in 2001 to combat rising insecurity. Notably, the government announced in mid-2001 that it would add more police officers and better equip the force, as well as improve training of customs officials.   Concerned about the impact small arms violence could have on the economy, especially the important tourism sector, it invited a delegation from the U.N. Department for Disarmament Affairs Conventional Arms

---

[61] E.M. Barine, Coordinator, Small Arms Unit, Kenyan Ministry of Foreign Affairs and International Cooperation, "Kenya: Small Arms Secretariat—Developments and Results," presentation at the BICC conference on "Curbing the Demand Side...," p. 2. By March 2002 a few of the signatories to the Nairobi Declaration had designated authorities responsible for follow-up (known as national focal points), but the problems described by the Kenyan official a year earlier remained barriers to progress.

[62] "Kenya: Government Cracks Down on Illegal Arms Imports," Integrated Regional Information Networks (IRIN), January 3, 2001.

[63] For example, an amnesty called in the North Rift area in April 2001 ultimately netted only one gun. Lucas Barasa and Marcus Barasa, "Moi's gun amnesty was ignored," *Daily Nation*, May 18, 2001. For a wider discussion of small arms demand see, for example, Quaker United Nations Offices (QUNO—New York and Geneva), "Curbing the Demand for Small Arms: Lessons in East Africa and the Horn of Africa," report of a conference held in Nairobi, December 12-16, 2000.

[64] "Government Gets Tough on Illegal Arms," PANA, February 14, 2001.   The proposed changes had not been adopted as of April 2002. Human Rights Watch email communication with J.A.N. Kamenju, Security Research and Information Centre, April 4, 2002.

Branch to conduct a fact-finding mission in Kenya in August 2001. These and other initiatives signal important progress achieved in a relatively short timeframe. Indeed, the Kenyan government is a leader in its region in recognizing the problem of small arms proliferation, as well as in working to coordinate a sub-regional response and implement a national strategy.

This positive momentum, however, has been marred by some misguided initiatives to control weapons flows, including the closing of the border with Somalia in 1999 and again in 2001, which while they were in place trapped asylum seekers, barred legitimate cross-border trade, and hampered the free movement of people. Moreover, the positive steps Kenya has taken have not been matched by advances in implementation to uphold existing law. In addition, actual and proposed measures fail to address the full scope of the small arms problem within Kenya.

To date, the government has not pursued a comprehensive approach to the widespread circulation and use of small arms. In particular, its emphasis on a legal and law enforcement-oriented strategy, with very limited attention to the factors driving demand for weapons—particularly insecurity deriving from ethnic tensions, the existence of armed community militias, and cross-border attacks, as well as poverty (aggravated by drought) and other socio-economic factors—holds little promise of addressing the problem in the systematic way required. The government has focused the blame for illegal arms on refugees. In diverting attention from its own responsibility, the government has ignored its role in permitting the transshipment of weapons throughout the region with inadequate controls. It also has failed to make the professionalization of the security forces a priority. Furthermore, by continuing to arm unaccountable police reservists and by neglecting to take action to address the dangerous role played by politicians who stoke communal conflict, the government itself contributes directly to the insecurity that drives small arms proliferation.

Part 2: Violence as a Political Tool in Kenya: The Case of the Coast

IV. VIOLENCE AS A POLITICAL TOOL IN KENYA

President Moi confidently predicted in 1991 that the introduction of multiparty politics in Kenya would result in ethnic violence.[65] His prediction has been alarmingly fulfilled. However, far from being the spontaneous result of a return to political pluralism, there is clear evidence that the government has been involved in provoking death, displacement, and terror among ethnic groups that are perceived to support the opposition.

The Politics of Division and Politically Motivated "Ethnic Clashes"

Political life in multiparty Kenya is largely defined along ethnic lines.[66] The association between ethnic identity and political affiliation in Kenya has provided the underlying logic for politically motivated ethnic violence. Often, the perpetrators of violence have been rallied around calls to introduce majimbo, a federal system of government based on ethnicity that could require the expulsion of all other ethnic groups from land occupied before the colonial period by the Kalenjin, Moi's own ethnic group, and other pastoral groups. While majimbo itself is a loose term translated as "federalism" or "regionalism" and need not imply the purging of non-indigenous groups, it has often been used to denote ethnically pure federalism. As explained in mid-1998 by the then-chair of the Law Society of Kenya, "majimbo does not exist in constitutional theory as a system of government. Its authors have the misconception that it is actually a federal system of government which, in addition to federalism as it is known ordinarily, also means the displacement of non-indigenous communities from their region to wherever they came from."[67]

---

[65] Human Rights Watch/Africa Watch, *Divide and Rule: State-Sponsored Ethnic Violence in Kenya* (New York: Human Rights Watch, 1993), p. 3.

[66] Kenya's population is made up of more than forty ethnic groups, the largest being (according to the 1989 census, the latest to provide a breakdown by ethnicity) the Kikuyu (21percent), Luhya (14 percent), Luo (13 percent), and Kalenjin (11 percent). Others include the Kisii (8 percent), Meru (5 percent), and Mijikenda (5 percent).

[67] Republic of Kenya, "Record of Evidence Taken Before the Judicial Commission of Inquiry into Tribal Clashes in Kenya (Verbatim Report)" (hereafter "Akiwumi Commission Official Transcript"), July 20, 1998.

The calls for such ethnically exclusive majimboism came initially in the early 1990s from Kalenjin and Maasai politicians.[68] These politicians proposed that the Rift Valley, which is allocated the largest number of seats in parliament, was traditionally Kalenjin/Maasai territory and that other ethnic groups living in the area should not be permitted to express differing political views in a multi-party system.

Using the language of majimbo, beginning in 1991, as Kenya prepared for its first-ever multiparty election the following year, ruling party politicians incited their ethnic-based supporters to drive away members of those groups that were expected to vote for opposition candidates. These clashes pitted the Kalenjin against the Luo, Luhya, and Kikuyu communities. High-ranking government officials were involved in the formation, training, and arming of so-called Kalenjin warriors. These warriors, wielding traditional weapons (mostly bows and arrows) and occasionally guns, carried out coordinated attacks on Kikuyu, Luhya, and Luo communities in Rift Valley, Western, and Nyanza provinces. These incidents of violence, which continued into the post-election period, claimed an estimated 1,500 lives and displaced at least 300,000 people. A cabinet minister was among the high-ranking KANU politicians found by a 1993 government inquiry and by Human Rights Watch to have been directly involved in instigating the politically-motivated ethnic violence of the early 1990s.[69] Top KANU figures were also implicated in the violence in testimony before a more recent government inquiry and asserted their innocence at that time.[70]

The general election that followed in December 1997 saw a return of politically motivated ethnic violence. In mid-1997, in the run-up to the election, armed raiders with backing from KANU party activists targeted potential opposition voters in weeks of pro-majimbo violent attacks in Kenya's Coast Province (see case study, below). Then, in early 1998, attacks in Rift Valley Province raised serious concerns that KANU supporters once again used violence

---

[68] In addition to the Kalenjin and Maasai, KANU (and previously KADU, Kenya African Democratic Union, which merged with KANU in the early 1960s) historically has represented other minority pastoral groups including the Turkana and Samburu communities.

[69] Human Rights Watch, *Divide and Rule*. A government-appointed parliamentary commission shared many of the same conclusions regarding government involvement in the "clashes." Republic of Kenya, *Report of the Parliamentary Select Committee to Investigate Ethnic Clashes in Western and Other Parts of Kenya* (Sept. 1993), known as the Kiliku Commission Report.

[70] Michael Njuguna and Watoro Kamau, "Five ministers send lawyers to Akiwumi Inquiry," *Daily Nation*, March 16, 1999.

to accomplish political objectives, this time to punish communities for their support of the opposition Democratic Party (DP). The violence was sparked just days after KANU politicians visited the area and threatened DP supporters. It also marked the first time the targeted Kikuyu community responded in an organized fashion with retaliatory attacks against Kalenjin communities.[71] Taken together, these incidents of politically-motivated ethnic violence have been estimated to have taken at least 2,000 lives and displaced over 400,000 people.[72]

In 1998 a presidential commission of inquiry was established to determine the causes of ethnic violence from 1991 to 1998 and to make specific recommendations, including for the prosecution of those found to be responsible. Known as the Akiwumi Commission, it took testimonies from over 200 witnesses around the country for a period of eleven months, focusing particular attention on the 1997 violence in Coast Province, discussed below.

Organized Political Attacks

Political debate among Kenya's fractured groups has often turned violent. This has taken the form of frequent skirmishes at political rallies, as well as targeted attacks on civic leaders or opposition politicians, particularly around election time or when political pressures are strong. In some cases, politicians have deliberately encouraged such political violence. The deputy police commissioner in 1998, Stephen Kimenchu, admitted that "powerful politicians" gave police officers orders to "clobber civilians and disperse peaceful demonstrations"; he withdrew his statement a few days later.[73]

Both the ruling party and opposition parties have informal civilian security groups, and KANU has unleashed bands of young supporters from the party's

---

[71] See Amnesty International, ARTICLE 19, and Human Rights Watch, "Kenya: Urgent Need for Action on Human Rights," press release, April 1998. For an account of the attacks, see Amnesty International, "Kenya: Political violence spirals," AI Index: AFR 32/019/1998, June 10, 1998.

[72] These figures have been derived from data about those incidents in Kenya Human Rights Commission (KHRC), *The Right to Return: The Internally Displaced Persons and the Culture of Impunity in Kenya* (Nairobi: Kenya Human Rights Commission, 2001). KHRC looked more broadly at state-sponsored or -condoned violence, in which it included additional incidents of inter-ethnic violence, and estimated that such violence had claimed over 4,000 lives and had displaced nearly 600,000 people from 1991 to 2001. Ibid.

[73] Judith Achieng, "Cleaning Up the Image of the Police," IPS, December 22, 1998; United States Department of State, *Country Reports on Human Rights Practices for 1999: Kenya* (Washington, DC: U.S. Government Printing Office, 1999), hereafter U.S. Department of State, *Country Reports 1999.*

youth wing to violently disrupt opposition-led rallies. For example, members of KANU's youth wing stabbed a photographer and beat a reporter in 1996 while (together with police) blocking opposition members from campaigning. KANU youth also reportedly were responsible for an attack on an opposition MP in April 1999. Later that year, the electoral commission wrote to the KANU secretary-general to urge that the party put an end to violence by party youths in a by-election campaign.[74]

One prominent pro-KANU security group formed of youths is called *Jeshi la Mzee* (the Old Man's Army). This gang of political thugs is notorious for intimidating and violently attacking opponents. Assistant Minister Fred Gumo, who has been accused of organizing and financing the group, has rejected such claims and denied any involvement in violent attacks attributed to *Jeshi la Mzee.*[75] In March 2002, acting in the wake of a wave of brutal killings in a Nairobi slum that left some twenty people dead, the government banned eighteen youth gangs and vigilante groups, including *Jeshi la Mzee.*[76]

Violent tactics have a long history in politics in Kenya's Coast Province as well. In 1993 Omar Masumbuko, a prominent KANU activist who had been the leader of the since disbanded Coast Youth for KANU '92, established the United Muslims of Kenya (UMKE), later renamed United Muslims of Africa (UMA). UMA was part of an organized effort by KANU intended to counter the influence of the nascent unregistered Islamic Party of Kenya (IPK). The apparent aim was to split Muslims of African descent from the allegedly Arab-dominated IPK. IPK supporters clashed with police and with UMA in 1993 and 1994, and in September 1994 KANU-backed UMA declared a *fatwa* against the IPK leader.[77]

According to a police statement attributed to a Coast politician, UMA's violent campaign against IPK was organized by KANU officials at the highest level and with the blessing of President Moi. In it, former KANU politician Emmanuel Karisa Maitha, who won a seat as an MP after defecting to the opposition in late

---

[74] Human Rights Watch, *Human Rights Watch World Report 1997* (New York: Human Rights Watch, 1996), p. 31; U.S. Department of State, *Country Reports 1999*; "Electoral body urges Kanu to end violence," *Daily Nation,* September 1, 1999.

[75] "Rev Njoya's assailant arrested as Gumo denies involvement," *Daily Nation,* June 15, 1999; "Alleged financier of secret terror-group ducks journalists," *Daily Nation,* June 14, 1999. See also U.S. Department of State, *Country Reports 1999.*

[76] "Banned groups were private armies for hire by politicians," *Daily Nation,* March 9, 2002.

[77] Human Rights Watch, *Human Rights Watch World Report 1994* (New York: Human Rights Watch, 1993), p. 23; Human Rights Watch, *Human Rights Watch World Report 1995* (New York: Human Rights Watch, 1994), p. 21.

1997, reportedly claimed he had first-hand knowledge about the UMA violence. The statement, which on its release Maitha strongly denied having written, reads in part:

> I have been involved in organising youth in the past who have organised operations which the State orders from time to time. These operations were always sanctioned by the DSC [District Security Committee] and PSC [Provincial Security Committee] where money is spent by the State agencies. I wish to elaborate further that sometime in the year 1991 to 1992 during the IPK resurgencies and disturbances at the Coast, I was called at [to] State House in Nairobi where I was engaged to [sic] a talk of how the IPK activities would be suppressed within Mombasa and at the Coast. Those who had been given the authority to tell me and who assured me they had the blessing of his Excellency the President was [sic] Mr. Joshua Kulei who is a personal assistant to the President and a Mr. Rashid Sajjad who is a nominated MP.[78]

According to his disputed statement, Maitha then arranged to recruit Omar Masumbuko to head up UMA and:

> Mr. Masumbuko usually could visit the State House alone or I would be called to go to Kulei or Mr. Sajjad for payment of any operation needed by the State. The DSC and PSC teams normally could be ordered to give us any help or even get logistic support from them. Despite all of this, I recall that Masumbuko managed to silence the IPK by various operations which included petrol bombing of targeted areas, fighting,

[78] The August 8, 1997, statement, which Maitha charged was fabricated by police and whose use was later blocked by order of the High Court, was read aloud in its entirety at the Akiwumi hearings by the officer who recorded it and who testified as to its authenticity. Akiwumi Commission Official Transcript, October 12, 1998, pp. 4-10, 20, 31. A copy of the statement also was reproduced in full in print. See Cautionary Statement Under Inquiry of Emmanuel Karisa Maitha, August 8, 1997, in MUHURI and KHRC, *Abandoned to Terror: Women and Violence at the Kenyan Coast* (Nairobi: Kenya Human Rights Commission, 2001). See also, Christine Pekeshe and Amadi Mugasia, "Kisauni MP denies writing any statement on violence," *East African Standard*, October 13, 1998.

invasion of Old Town [a neighborhood in Mombasa] and hijacking of Khalid Balala and others. I wish to state further that after the silencing of the IPK, UMA was disbanded with the instructions from State House, where most of the youths and their leaders were paid or some were employed for the good jobs they had done. I was approached again in the year 1993 where I [was] asked now to reassemble the UMA youth who were now already trained so that they could be ordered to do a further State Operation. When ordered I assembled all the youth leaders and I changed the name from UMA to Coast Protective Group (CPG). I was under the paymaster of Kulei and Sajjad.[79]

The statement went on to name various operations carried out with the organized youth, including the disruption of opposition political rallies, and to address other topics.

Maitha repudiated the statement and its contents, saying he had never been involved with UMA or Masumbuko.[80] Sajjad denied he had financed UMA, and also denied that Kulei had been linked to Maitha.[81] A statement by Masumbuko, however, does not support these denials and instead confirms the information in the statement attributed to Maitha concerning high-level political involvement in the violent UMA campaign.[82]

---

[79] Akiwumi Commission Official Transcript, October 12, 1998, pp. 6-10. Notably, some of the same politicians mentioned in the disputed statement were also implicated in the 1997 Coast violence. See below.

[80] Ibid., pp. 119-20; Akiwumi Commission Official Transcript, October 13, 1998, pp. 81, 103-5, 125.

[81] J. Sekoh-Ochieng, "Likoni: Sajjad gave Sh400,000," *Daily Nation*, October 22, 1998; Maguta Kimemia and J. Sekoh-Ochieng, "How we bought votes, by Sajjad," *Daily Nation*, October 23, 1998.

[82] The existence of Masumbuko's statement and the sensitive nature of its content was noted in police testimony several times at the Akiwumi Commission. See, for example, Akiwumi Commission Official Transcript, October 14, 1998, pp. 76-78; and Akiwumi Commission Official Transcript, June 9, 1999, pp. 54-55. This testimony also referred several times to the August 24, 1997, report by then-Senior Assistant Commissioner of Police Edwin Nyaseda (entered into evidence as Exhibit 82), which described Maitha and Masumbuko as persons with involvement in "helping the Government in fighting political enemies" in the early 1990s. Akiwumi Commission Official Transcript, October 14, 1998, pp. 76-78.

V. CASE STUDY: ARMED POLITICAL VIOLENCE
ON THE COAST

Violence erupted on Kenya's coast on August 13, 1997, launching weeks of terror in what had been a quiet resort area. Using the cover of automatic guns wielded by outsiders, local raiders carrying traditional weapons attacked a police station and a police post at the ferry in Likoni, which connects Likoni to Mombasa island. The raiders killed six officers and stole more than forty guns, then proceeded to carry out a violent rampage in the area, burning market kiosks, office buildings, and killing and maiming people after identifying them as non-locals or people from "up-country." Many of their targets belonged to the Luo, Luhya, or Kikuyu communities, as well as the Kamba. Some two hundred raiders participated in the attack, by the raiders' own count. When security forces finally appeared the following morning, the raiders retreated to hiding places in the forests. From these bases, they launched more attacks in subsequent days and engaged in sporadic firefights with security forces. The violence continued for several weeks, with particularly bold attacks taking place again in September, before they subsided. Intermittent raids continued well into November 1997 and some raiders were active through December of the following year.

The impact of the violence was devastating. Statistics compiled by the police, which provide a conservative estimate, indicate that a total of 104 people were killed in the violence, at least 133 more were injured, hundreds of structures were damaged, and other property was damaged or stolen leading to large losses.[83] Human rights groups estimate that, in addition to more than a hundred people killed, some 100,000 people were displaced. Furthermore, the Coast region's lucrative tourism trade came to a virtual stand-still overnight, and the country as a whole experienced a sharp downturn in tourism following the violence.

Echoes of Rwanda

The methods employed in Rwanda's genocide were replicated on a much smaller but still deadly scale in Kenya. In Rwanda, politicians exploited ethnic divisions to preserve and expand their own power. They accused a group of "foreigners" of supporting the political opposition on the basis merely of similar ethnic identification. They mobilized supporters to carry out acts of targeted violence for which they granted them complete impunity. They used a party-based

---

[83] Akiwumi Commission Official Transcript, July 21, 1998, p.23. According to these figures, ten police officers and thirty-seven raiders were among those killed, and nineteen police officers and at least eight raiders were injured.

youth group, the Interahamwe militia, to carry out the first attacks and later created a paramilitary system of "civilian self-defense" where ordinary citizens were guided by political leaders and trained and armed by soldiers, former soldiers, and police.[84]

Although the central importance of firearms is often overlooked, the state-organized violence against Tutsi in Rwanda shows the deadly effect of joining firearms to political violence. Both before and during the genocide, killers were able to kill faster and more easily because they were armed with guns and grenades. After the genocide, bullet shells were found littering the ground at massacre sites. Soldiers, militia, or ordinary citizens who had gotten their firearms from the authorities launched the major massacres, each of which killed thousands of people. In the space of one hundred days, assailants slaughtered at least half a million persons. Assailants with firearms enjoyed an enormous advantage over their unarmed victims, in psychological as well as in real terms. So great was the terror created by firearms that those targeted were often paralyzed into inaction, leaving them easy prey for later waves of assailants who were armed only with machetes, clubs, or other home-made weapons. Used in this manner as an instrument of terror, guns contributed to deaths on an astounding scale in Rwanda.[85] In the hands of the raiders in Kenya's Coast Province, they would contribute to shocking chaos and bloodshed.

Origins of the 1997 Violence: The Manipulation of Volatile Local Conditions

Conditions in Coast Province in 1997 provided fertile ground for fomenting politically motivated ethnic violence. Life had long been harsh for the ethnic groups that were traditional inhabitants of the area. The indigenous Mijikenda people of the Coast (comprising the Digo, Giriama, and other ethnic groups) lived in poverty, surrounded by resort hotels catering to foreign and Kenyan tourists. The Digos, mostly concentrated south of Mombasa (in the area known as the South Coast), had disproportionately high rates of joblessness, landlessness, and illiteracy in comparison with members of non-local ethnic groups living in the same area,

---

[84] Human Rights Watch and Federation Internationale des Ligues des Droits de l'Homme (FIDH), *Leave None to Tell the Story: Genocide in Rwanda* (New York: Human Rights Watch, 1999), especially pp. 3-5, 223-237; Human Rights Watch, *Playing the "Communal Card": Communal Violence and Human Rights* (New York: Human Rights Watch, 1995), pp. viii-xi.

[85] Human Rights Watch and FIDH, *Leave None to Tell the Story*, especially pp. 4-6, 8-9, 336, 649-653.

which included so-called up-country people (members of ethnic groups from Kenya's interior, generally viewed as opposition supporters) and residents of Arab and Asian descent, many of whom had long family histories in the Coast region. Beach-front properties and other valuable land, including Mijikenda ancestral land, were in the hands of wealthy foreigners and politically connected Kenyans, some of whom allegedly obtained the deeds irregularly in a practice known as land-grabbing. Added to their anger over these inequities, many locals were upset over abuse suffered at the hands of police officers, whom they said arrested young men without cause, beat them, and demanded large, unaffordable bribes in order to release them.[86]

KANU politicians astutely turned local bitterness into political support for their party. As in other parts of Kenya, such as the Rift Valley, they rallied the local population around calls for majimbo, the federal system promising the return of land to the control of its pre-colonial inhabitants and that regions would gain greater autonomy vis-à-vis the central government (see above). The majimboist argument resonated well with the local population. As one indicator, Coast Province voted overwhelmingly for KANU in the 1992 elections.[87] By emphasizing that the purging of non-local people would permit the indigenous Digos and other Mijikendas to attain all that was left behind, pro-majimbo KANU politicians helped make the up-country people residing among them, rather than their own leaders and the government, the focus of local anger.

Some members of the Digo community were keenly aware that one way to achieve majimbo was to use intimidation and violence to expel non-indigenous residents. This had been the lesson of the violence in parts of western Kenya that began in 1991, when majimbo was a lightning rod for politically instigated "ethnic" clashes in Rift Valley and neighboring provinces. This lesson had already been applied in the Coast region prior to 1997. In fact, in the early 1990s, as the Rift Valley violence was underway, a group of Digos attempted to use the same tactics on a smaller scale in the Likoni area.[88]

Speaking to Human Rights Watch, a Digo man who participated in the earlier Likoni violence said the attacks were part of a pro-majimbo strategy. He asserted

---

[86] Human Rights Watch interviews, Coast Province, April and May 1999; KHRC, *Kayas of Deprivation, Kayas of Blood: Violence, Ethnicity and the State in Coastal Kenya* (Nairobi: Kenya Human Rights Commission, 1997).

[87] To give local expression to their majimboist sentiments, some Digo leaders formed new political movements in Coast Province, as noted below.

[88] While some published sources agree that pro-majimbo attacks took place in 1992, as described to Human Rights Watch by raiders, others refer to violence in 1993.

that local Digo leaders organized area youth to take an oath to attack up-country residents and thus bring about majimbo, but that the recruits went wild after the oathing ceremony instead of waiting as instructed.[89] Another raider referred to the earlier attacks, stating, "1997 wasn't the first time. In 1992 we were told the same thing—to chase the Luos away."[90]

In testimony to the Akiwumi Commission, a witness named Joseph Ochwangi Onyiego, a resident of the Matuga area of Kwale district, stated that at a November 1991 public meeting his local councillor, of the ruling KANU party, advocated majimbo and incited violence against up-country residents by warning that up-country people who supported the opposition in the upcoming election would be attacked as in Molo, Rift Valley Province, with "arrows in their backs."[91]

Local conditions in the Coast region had long been poor, but in 1997 the national political backdrop again helped set the stage for violence. Non-locals were expected to vote against KANU in elections in December of that year, when the party hoped to win back parliamentary seats it had lost to the opposition in the first multiparty election, held in 1992, as well as prevent further electoral losses and undermine support for opposition parties. Up-country voters were concentrated in areas KANU had lost in the 1992 election and that it wished to regain. KANU also needed to win at least 25 percent of the Coast Province vote as a whole to ensure the reelection of President Moi. In addition, at the national level political tensions were rising as opposition parties and civic groups criticized KANU over its intransigence on constitutional reform and organized large pro-reform rallies. Fourteen people were reported killed in violence at pro-reform rallies in July 1997, and further deaths followed in the first half of August.[92] In Coast Province, a KANU politician allegedly threatened violence against pro-reform demonstrators.[93]

At the Akiwumi hearings, Onyiego stated that KANU laid the political groundwork for the 1997 violence. He said that KANU leaders strongly promoted

---

[89] Human Rights Watch interview with Raider B, Ukunda (Coast Province), May 8, 1999. All interviews with raiders were conducted individually and in private. Two raiders were interviewed twice on different dates.

[90] Human Rights Watch interview with Raider F, Mombasa (Coast Province), May 24, 1999.

[91] Akiwumi Commission Official Transcript, August 28, 1998, p. 2; Amadi Mugasia, "Raiders' military training alleged," *East African Standard*, August 29, 1998; Michael Mumo and Patrick Mayoyo, "Security 'notified of raids," *Daily Nation*, August 29, 1998. In press accounts, the witness's name was spelled Onyigo.

[92] Louise Tunbridge, "Gang kills five in Mombasa slum," *Daily Telegraph* (London), August 18, 1997.

[93] Human Rights Watch interviews with two eyewitnesses, Mombasa, May 1999.

majimbo in the Coast region and that this had the effect of stoking local anger and inciting violence against the up-country people, including in meetings held just prior to the Likoni attack. The witness said that on August 10, 1997, three days before the attack, he attended a public meeting held by KANU MP Boy Juma Boy (see below), who said he was campaigning for votes. Onyiego alleged that the Coast MP told those gathered that up-country residents were taking all the money from local jobs and tourism while local people were unemployed.[94] Onyiego also testified that Boy explicitly called for majimbo, saying it was what the people from the Coast region wanted, as did other leaders at the meetings.[95] Two local-level officials testified about public meetings Boy held in Onyiego's area in July 1997 (Onyiego had spoken of August) and both denied that there was incitement at them.[96] Boy, who also testified as to the allegations, strongly rejected Onyiego's testimony.[97]

When the Likoni violence broke out, it emerged that "[i]n recent months several ruling party politicians have exhorted Mombasans to force outside groups back up country."[98] At the Akiwumi hearings, a police officer said he received complaints prior to August 1997 that Boy had incited local residents against their up-country neighbors.[99] A second policeman testified that an informer who attended oathing ceremonies in April 1997 said he had seen Boy, together with KANU MP colleague Kassim Mwamzandi, at the oathing site in the area north of

---

[94] Akiwumi Commission Official Transcript, August 27, 1998, pp. 56-58.

[95] Ibid; Akiwumi Commission Official Transcript, August 28, 1998, p. 3-4. Accounts of the meeting, as described by the witness, were also reported in the press. See Patrick Mayoyo and Michael Mumo, "Inquiry told of night meeting," Daily Nation, August 28, 1998; Mugasia, "Raiders' military...," East African Standard; Mumo and Mayoyo, "Security 'notified of raids," Daily Nation. Boy Juma Boy's name is variously abbreviated in official documents and press reports as Boy or Juma Boy. We adopt the former usage, in part to avoid confusion over Boy Juma Boy's father, a politician whose name was Juma Boy.

[96] Akiwumi Commission Official Transcript, August 28, 1998, p. 23; Akiwumi Commission Official Transcript, August 31, 1998, p. 55-62.

[97] Akiwumi Commission Official Transcript, October 23, 1998, pp. 17-20.

[98] Stephen Buckley, "Explosion of violence in Kenya stirs fears of electoral mayhem," International Herald Tribune, August 21, 1997.

[99] "Muslim youth invaded Diani police station, witness says," East African Standard, September 15, 1998; Patrick Mayoyo and Michael Mumo, "Witchcraft cited at hearing," Daily Nation, September 15, 1998.

Mombasa known as the North Coast.[100] According to the police officer, the local organizer of the oathing ceremonies admitted his role and explained to police that the oath was to motivate local men to fight for land.[101] Boy, for his part, vehemently denied that he had been present at the oathing site in 1997.[102]

Allegations of the use of inflammatory rhetoric went back even further. In a November 1994 incident described in the press, Mwamzandi reportedly threatened that he would "order my people to demolish [the market kiosks of up-country people] immediately" and fellow MP Boy reportedly warned non-indigenous residents of the Coast that "danger is looming."[103] A police officer who testified before the Akiwumi Commission indicated that in her opinion the statements constituted "a summons of war," yet no action was taken against the two politicians or the then-provincial commissioner (holder of the top Coast Province administration position), who presided over the meeting.[104] Boy denied that he had ever incited indigenous groups against up-country residents.[105]

The young Digo men who were recruited to join the Coast raiders in 1997 told Human Rights Watch that their primary motivation was obtaining access to their ancestral lands, property, and jobs. They agreed to use violence to expel up-country residents because—having been inculcated with the politically charged rhetoric of majimbo—they strongly believed such acts were justified and necessary for the advancement of themselves and their community. Even though they were aware that KANU politicians in the Coast region promoted majimbo, the raiders made clear that they did not pursue a strategy of violent expulsion in order to improve the party's electoral prospects. Afterwards, however, when they were discarded and abandoned by KANU, the realization sank in that they and their cause had been manipulated to serve the interests of KANU in the run-up to the elections without any real concern for the welfare of the Digo people.

---

[100] Akiwumi Commission Official Transcript, October 9, 1998, pp. 3-5; Patrick Mayoyo and Robert Nyaga, "Ex-MPs attended oathing, clashes inquiry told," *Daily Nation*, October 10, 1998.

[101] Akiwumi Commission Official Transcript, October 9, 1998, pp. 3-5; Patrick Mayoyo and Robert Nyaga, "Ex-MPs attended oathing, clashes inquiry told," *Daily Nation*, October 10, 1998.

[102] Akiwumi Commission Official Transcript, October 23, 1998, pp. 70-71.

[103] Patrick Mayoyo, "Leaders warn 'foreigners,'" *Daily Nation*, November 4, 1994. See also Michael Mumo and Ngumbao Kithi, "Inquiry told of altered journals," *Daily Nation*, September 25, 1998.

[104] Amadi Mugasia, "Raid suspect held," *East African Standard*, September 2, 1998.

[105] Akiwumi Commission Official Transcript, October 23, 1998, pp. 71, 130.

The first-hand testimonies of the raiders provide important insights into state involvement in the Coast violence. Together with sworn testimony given before the Akiwumi Commission, the testimonies of the raiders make clear that—at a minimum—KANU politicians and government officials took a number of steps to facilitate the raiders' activities and to protect them from being held accountable for their actions. In addition, the raiders' testimonies suggest that the involvement of politicians may have been much deeper. Several raiders asserted that people identified as KANU MPs, candidates, and activists visited the raiders and met with their commanders and a spiritual leader who served as a key advisor. The raiders alleged that some of these politicians delivered food, money—even guns, according to one raider—and otherwise supported their cause. Looking back at the events in 1997, the raiders have since come to believe that top Coast Province political leaders, working with local interlocutors, orchestrated the events from behind the scenes to benefit the government of President Moi. This interpretation also accords with other testimonies suggesting that prominent KANU politicians were involved in the plot to spark violence in Coast Province. The implicated politicians, for their part, uniformly deny sponsoring the raiders. In most cases, they reject claims that they visited the raiders, and others provide alternative explanations for the assistance they provided, often indirectly, to raiders.

The names of several politicians feature repeatedly in the testimonies given at the Akiwumi Commission on the Coast Province violence. They are, in alphabetical order:

Boy Juma Boy: The MP for Matuga (KANU) at the time of the raids and also Chief Whip for the party in parliament. Later in 1997 Boy lost the KANU nomination to another candidate, Suleiman Kamole.

Suleiman Kamole (or Kamolleh): A candidate for parliament on the KANU ticket in 1997. In December that year he was elected MP for Matuga, the seat previously held by Boy.

Emmanuel Karisa Maitha: A KANU politician at the time of the violence. He defected to the opposition Democratic Party after losing the KANU primary in November 1997 and won the race for MP for Kisauni the following month. He ran as the KANU candidate for the Kisauni MP seat in the previous general election, in 1992.

Mwalimu Masoud Mwahima: A KANU councillor and also KANU chairman for Likoni in 1997. Mwahima later became Mombasa's deputy mayor and then mayor, a position he holds as of early 2002.

Kassim Mwamzandi: MP for Msambweni (KANU) and an assistant minister at the time of the Likoni raid in mid-1997. He hoped to be reelected, but was defeated for the KANU nomination in late 1997.

Rashid Sajjad: The KANU campaign coordinator for Coast Province for the 1997 elections. He also served as a nominated (appointed, rather than elected) MP for KANU and an assistant minister in the Moi government. As of this writing he remains an MP and government assistant minister.

Suleiman Rashid Shakombo: A KANU candidate for the MP seat for Likoni. After losing the KANU nomination for the seat to another candidate, he defected to the newly formed Shirikisho Party of Kenya (SPK) in November 1997. Shakombo ran for parliament on the SPK ticket and won in the general election, becoming MP.

Orchestration of the Violence

KANU Allies Recruit Raiders "for a Political Mission"

In the first quarter of 1997, organizers of the violence began a clandestine recruiting campaign among the area's indigenous population. Young men in their twenties and thirties were approached by local leaders, invited to take part in violent attacks, and promised rewards for their participation. South of Mombasa, for example, an influential local businessman rounded up young men, told them they would receive training to enable them to drive out the up-country people, and promised them he would help them get the houses and jobs left behind. He also gave each of the recruits, a group of some twenty-five young men, some money (Ksh.500 or $8.50) and transported them to the training camp.[106]

This businessman allegedly coordinated recruitment in the Likoni area with a councillor who also served as the KANU chairman in that area, Mwalimu Masoud Mwahima, whom raiders who defected said recruited them and who was otherwise alleged to have supported the raiders' activities. Mwahima, who later became Mombasa's deputy mayor and eventually mayor, strenuously denied the

---

[106] Human Rights Watch interview with Raider A, Ukunda, April 22, 1999.

charges, saying he had no prior knowledge of the planned raids and was not involved in the violence.[107]

Other local-level politicians participated in the recruitment effort. Near the border with Tanzania, for example, an area councillor called groups of young men together and encouraged them to join efforts to chase away the up-country people, in return for which they would each be given a house.[108] A councillor in a different area was also alleged to have actively recruited young men to join the raiders and otherwise to have participated in the organization of the violence.[109]

One raider, a veteran of the 1992 Likoni violence, joined of his own initiative after becoming frustrated that KANU was not able to do more to address landlessness in the area. In 1997, he traveled as far as the North Coast town of Malindi to attract recruits and prepare the ground for a new round of violence. He sought in particular to recruit men who had previously served in the military or police, and also reached out to active-duty Digo servicemen based in the area. He said: "We wanted just a hundred key people, strong ones. [...] When we were planning, we sent message to Digos and other Mijikenda—our brothers—in the barracks who were still serving with the government. We called those serving near home and they got oathed."[110]

This raider claimed to have high-level KANU contacts, saying he had at least two powerful friends among KANU politicians in Coast Province. He said an MP had earlier arranged for him to be released on bond (and paid the bond) after the young man was arrested and charged with trespassing for illegally occupying land owned by an up-country farmer. The same KANU leader encouraged the young man to go back and continue to illegally farm on that land. In addition, the raider said he had helped another important KANU friend get elected to a parliamentary seat. He stated, "I have opened doors for these politicians to get where they are, and now they forget me."[111]

---

[107] KHRC, *Kayas of Deprivation*, pp. 22-23; KHRC, *Kayas Revisited: A Post-Election Balance Sheet* (Nairobi: Kenya Human Rights Commission, 1998), pp. 11-16. The official's name also has appeared as Masoud Mwahima and Mwalimu Masoud Mwaluma. "Mwalimu" is an honorific in Swahili meaning "teacher." Mwahima was later arrested in connection with the Likoni violence and released under unclear circumstances. See below.

[108] Human Rights Watch interview with Raider F, Mombasa, May 24, 1999.

[109] KHRC, *Kayas Revisited*, p. 2, 17; Law Society of Kenya, "A Report of the Massacre/Violence in Coast Province," October 1997, p. 10.

[110] Human Rights Watch interview with Raider B, Ukunda, May 8, 1999.

[111] Ibid.

Beyond his own ties to the ruling party, the veteran raider mentioned other ways in which the raiders' recruitment drive was associated with KANU. He said that he approached young men whom he knew had taken part in the United Muslims of Africa (UMA), a group closely linked to KANU that was known for violence in the Coast region (see above), and successfully recruited them to join the raiders' effort. He added that Juma Bempa, a lead organizer who was to become the raiders' military leader, had political ties to KANU: "Bempa privately met with politicians before the attack," but "[i]t was a secret. [...] After the 1992 clashes, Bempa tried to be a councillor for Likoni on the KANU ticket, and in 1997 it [the violence] was his plan. He told us he was addressing people in a secret way."[112]

Much of the recruitment happened by word of mouth, drawing on the anger of local young men over their poverty, unemployment, landlessness, and poor educational opportunities, and the prevalent sentiment that up-country people were to blame. Rumors quickly circulated among the Digo community of the South Coast that something was afoot, and that men were receiving basic military training. Hearing that a local traditional healer named Swaleh Salim bin Alfan was holding oathing ceremonies and encouraging willing recruits to attend, many went to his house to volunteer.[113] As one recruit stated, "Recruitment was easy because people were talking anyway. The time was ripe for people to stand up. Word spread by word of mouth that to be involved you should go to Swaleh's house."[114] At least one young man from the area near Alfan's home said he was recruited directly by the spiritual leader.[115]

It is clear from testimonies that there was a strong political dimension to the recruitment campaign. The new recruits, regardless of who first approached them, said that they were told the purpose of the raids was to bring majimbo to the Coast region. One individual who was recruited to join the raiders, but did not take part in the violence, stated: "The people were told that this effort was for majimbo. The song was always majimbo and majimbo only."[116] A raider said that the area councillor who recruited him told him that "people wanted to start majimbo...[O]nce we chased away the up-country people we would have the area,

---

[112] Human Rights Watch interview with Raider B, Mombasa, May 26, 1999. Bempa's name has appeared as "Bemba" in some press reports.

[113] Human Rights Watch interviews with Raider C, Raider D, and Raider E, Mombasa, May 1999. Alfan's name sometimes appears in other publications as Swalehe Halfani.

[114] Human Rights Watch interview with Raider E, Mombasa, May 9, 1999.

[115] Human Rights Watch interview with Raider C, Mombasa, May 9, 1999.

[116] Human Rights Watch interview with Raider E, Mombasa, May 9, 1999.

we would take control."[117] The veteran raider said the effort to organize violence in 1997 was a continuation of the attacks in 1992, when he had first been approached "for a political mission" to bring majimbo to the Coast.[118]

There was never any doubt that the recruits were being asked to use violent means and intimidation to achieve their goals. As one of them put it, "It was already known from the Rift Valley how to chase people out—by clashes—so it was copied. The idea was to organize the youth to evict up-country people."[119] The same person explained, "If you say 'majimbo,' you mean driving non-indigenous people out."

One raider said that, after he was recruited, he was told by the raiders' leaders that they would time their attacks to coincide with the dissolution of parliament, which marks the beginning of the presidential campaign. He added, "We were to attack in areas where up-country people are concentrated."[120] No other raiders who spoke to Human Rights Watch said they were aware at the time that the planned violence was linked to the election campaign; however, two defected raiders who spoke to the Kenya Human Rights Commission (KHRC) indicated they knew there was a connection between their actions and the elections, saying they were given this information by their leaders.[121]

The raiders who spoke to Human Rights Watch were in their mid-twenties to late thirties. While they often referred to their fellow recruits as "the boys," they clarified that only adults were permitted to join them. They acknowledged, however, that many in the Digo community, including children, sympathized with their cause and sought to show support. In some cases, "small boys" (youths seventeen years old and younger) helped deliver food to the raiders, and local women and children at the sites where the raiders struck sometimes rallied behind the raiders during attacks. Contrary to the raiders' accounts, however, at least one police official declared that children as young as fourteen took part in attacks.[122]

---

[117] Human Rights Watch interview with Raider F, Mombasa, May 24, 1999.

[118] The raider said he joined the raiders even though by 1997 he no longer felt majimbo was enough to preserve the interest of indigenous residents of the Coast and wanted to fight for the region's independence. The raiders' leaders, he said, explicitly rejected his broader agenda. Human Rights Watch interview with Raider B, Ukunda, May 8, 1999.

[119] Human Rights Watch interview with Raider E, Mombasa, May 9, 1999.

[120] Human Rights Watch interview with Raider A, Mombasa, May 21, 1999.

[121] In one case the raider received this information from a military leader, in another from a person who recruited for the raiders. KHRC, *Kayas of Deprivation*, pp. 22-24.

[122] Akiwumi Commission Official Transcript, July 21, 1998, p. 17; Gichuru Njihia and Maguta Kimemia, "Raiders 'took oath' against non-coastals," *Daily Nation*, July 22, 1998.

Oathing: Using Tradition to Organize Political Violence

After being recruited to perpetrate violent attacks, the young men were taken to local spiritual leaders to undergo so-called ritual oathing in connection with the planned raids. The oathings greatly facilitated the military-style organization of the violence, in particular by bringing together the young men who had agreed to participate in the raids, motivating them to perform their task, binding them to a culturally important vow of secrecy and allegiance, and providing an opportunity for their leaders to organize them into units and convey orders.[123] The oath committed the young men who took it to carry out the mission for which they had been recruited, and to keep this mission a secret, in exchange for which they were promised supernatural protection from harm.[124]

One recruit who took the oath explained:

> The oath is to make you strong and unafraid; it's for taking action. There were instructions about what not to do that day (sleep on a bed, for example). The oath protects you from being caught. Your enemy can't see you. It also protects you from getting hurt. It lasts until you do things that aren't allowed. You're only safe to do the action you're told to do. For this oath, the task was to evict the up-country people.[125]

Oathing ceremonies took place at various locations in the province for months leading up to the August 13th attack at Likoni and continued afterwards as new recruits joined. Almost all of the raiders who spoke to Human Rights Watch indicated that Alfan administered the oaths to them, and that he did so at his residence on the South Coast near the edge of the Kaya Bombo forest.[126] In Digo belief, forests or "kayas" are home to spirits and therefore considered holy places.

The oath administered to the recruits was called a "kinu oath." From what the raiders described, the ceremony involves an overturned clay pot or "kinu." Those taking the oath form a line and are given small cuts in various places with razors,

---

[123] Human Rights Watch interviews with Raider A, Raider B, Raider C, Raider D, Raider E, and Raider F, Coast Province, April and May 1999.

[124] The raiders believed the oath protected them from bullets and might make them invisible to their opponents. Human Rights Watch interviews with Raider B and Raider E, Coast Province, April and May 1999.

[125] Human Rights Watch interview with Raider E, Mombasa, May 9, 1999.

[126] Human Rights Watch interviews with Raider A, Raider B, Raider C, Raider D, and Raider E, Coast Province, April and May 1999.

leaving scars that were still clearly visible two years later. Medicinal herbs are rubbed into the fresh cuts made on the skin. The oathing ceremony generally takes place under a baobab tree, which has special religious significance.[127]

Several raiders spoke of the oathing ceremony, and the powerful effect it had on them. In one raider's words:

> At Mzee Swaleh's house there were about 170 men. We were put into groups according to where we were from [...]. Then we were all administered with an oath. Cuts were made on our tongue, our temple, the left hand at the edge of the little finger. Medicine was applied to our skin. We were given nothing to eat. There was a line of people and there were two people (Swaleh's assistants) administering the oaths one by one. Mzee Swaleh was watching seated. We were told that the up-country people had taken everything and that it was time to rise up against this unfairness. After taking the oath we felt agitated and strong. We wanted to take action immediately, but we were told to wait.[128]

On another occasion a raider described the night of his oathing:

> In March 1997 I was approached by [Swaleh bin] Alfan who told me that we needed to get together to protect our rights. Around that time, I went to Swaleh's house and under the baobab tree at night I took an oath. There were about 200 people who were oathed one by one. We would be called under the tree to oath and then would leave and sit outside in the compound. The oathing went from 7 p.m. to 7 a.m. It took about ten minutes a person. After the oath I felt strong. We were told to wait by Swaleh. "We will call you in August," he said, "and explain further." We were told to demand for our rights. We were told to get the up-country people out. We were

---

[127] One raider said the pot has a dead chicken inside it, along with pieces of cloth in red, black, and white.

[128] Human Rights Watch interview with Raider D, Mombasa, May 9, 1999. "Mzee" is used as a term of respect.

told to wait because we don't have the weapons yet. We were
divided into groups and told to wait until August.[129]

Swaleh bin Alfan denied that he had administered any oaths to raiders, telling
Human Rights Watch, "What was said about me oathing raiders was a lie." He also
rejected press accounts characterizing him as a "witchdoctor" and "medicineman."
While stating that he had "special powers," he clarified, "I don't use them against
people unless someone comes around to cause problems. I use my power to help
people and not to inflict any injury."[130]

As the raiders explained, after the oathing ceremonies their leaders divided
them into groups or units to receive further instruction. While hundreds of young
men took the oath, not all joined their ranks. A large number were simply
sympathizers who supported the raiders' cause but did not want to fight and
therefore did not join the groups that were formed. Of those who were prepared
to fight, some were told simply to wait, while the leaders ordered others to gather
for informal military training. As one of the raiders stated, they were told only a
hundred good fighters were required to be effective.[131]

Command Structure, Discipline, and Order

Following the successful recruitment and oathing campaigns, the raiders'
leaders further extended the military model of organization to determine the overall
structure of the newly-created force. A chain of command existed whereby a
handful of ethnic Digo men conveyed orders to the raiders. The local leaders,
sometimes called "group leaders," had taken a lead in the recruiting drive. Most
of them had once served as members of the Kenyan armed forces or police. The
small committee of leaders was headed by a dynamic ex-military man named Juma
Bempa. They were joined by a group of highly trained and well-armed men
described as "soldiers," whom the raiders also referred to as "outsiders" (see
below). Together, the local leaders and these soldiers exercised military command
over the raiders, with Bempa usually taking the lead and generally considered the
overall military commander. The other local leaders and soldiers were responsible
for training.[132]

---

[129] Human Rights Watch interview with Raider C, Mombasa, May 9, 1999.
[130] Human Rights Watch interview with Swaleh bin Alfan, Denyenye (Coast
Province), May 25, 1999.
[131] Human Rights Watch interview with Raider B, Ukunda, May 8, 1999.
[132] Human Rights Watch interviews with Raider A, Raider B, Raider C, Raider D, and
Raider F, Coast Province, April and May 1999.

As noted, those with prior military experience were especially sought-after recruits. Some recruits were active-duty members of the armed services. However, not all of those with Kenyan armed services experience were given a leadership role. Some were rank-and-file raiders.

The raiders interviewed agreed that Swaleh bin Alfan exercised significant responsibilities beyond his role as their spiritual leader. He carried out most of the oathing ceremonies on the South Coast, where the raiders were based, and maintained very close contact with the raiders' military leaders. In addition, Alfan offered instruction, advice, and material support (including food and money). Several raiders also indicated that Alfan was the interlocutor between the raiders' commanders and important KANU politicians whom they witnessed visiting him at his home and who they said provided food and other assistance, often via Alfan (see below).

One young man who said he did not take part in any attacks but who was recruited to join the raiders and had access to information because he lived near Alfan explained the hierarchy of power: "Bempa was the commander. He'd take instructions from the elders and then manage his boys. Actually, Swaleh was the senior elder, and was the master, so Bempa took instructions from him. Bempa would come to Swaleh's house every day during the daytime."[133] He, like several other raiders, emphasized that Bempa's qualities made him well-suited to be the raider's military leader, adding that the decision was made by Alfan: "Bempa was selected as the leader because he was an ex-serviceman who was brave. He was hardcore. People liked him and the old man [Alfan] picked him as the commander."[134] A raider who was an early recruit also asserted that Alfan had selected Bempa to be the raiders' military leader.[135]

In keeping with their military structure, the raiders took steps to ensure discipline and organization. For the sake of secrecy, they were not supposed to refer to their leaders or each other by name. The group leaders and Bempa, however, seemed less concerned about concealing their identity than the soldiers, and the recruits came to learn their names. Early recruits also explained that the leaders recorded the names of the raiders in a register and kept military and other records. Each of them was assigned a code name or number to conceal his identity. Their real names and the code given to them were copied into the register, described by one as "a black book with a hard cover and a red spine," that began

---

[133] Human Rights Watch interview with Raider E, Mombasa, May 9, 1999.
[134] Ibid.
[135] Human Rights Watch interview with Raider B, Mombasa, May 26, 1999.

to be used before the raids started.[136] A different raider gave a more complete explanation. He said: "There was a book with our records. It was captured by the police [...] near Kaya Bombo. It had names, budgets, letters [...]. All our arrangements—how to budget for food and record of arms and [also listed] the numbers and names of all of us. [...] We also had papers with the names of people assigned for different operations."[137]

The police later recovered materials fitting that description. A police officer who viewed the materials said there were actually two books and that the first included entries from August 19 to September 11 and documented military information. It showed that there were 278 raiders at that time and provided a "force number" for each of them next to their names. It also indicated that Juma Bempa was the commanding officer and that the raiders were divided into different "companies" of fixed composition, and listed the dates of the training given to each group. The officer said the second book contained information of a more logistical nature and was recovered at the same time. She described it as including an attendance register, records of personnel matters (promotions and demotions, disciplinary actions), and a firearms register that detailed the number of guns, their serial numbers, and a log of who used them. According to her, the number of guns listed matched the number stolen from the police. Finally, she said, the second book detailed the raiders' expenses on food and hospital treatment and included an unsent letter. She did not mention whether it contained information on the financing of the group, as would later be speculated.[138]

The then-head of criminal investigations for Coast Province (PCIO) was involved in the arrest of Swaleh bin Alfan and several others in an operation on August 15. He stated that at that time officers recovered a notebook and photographic negatives from one of the people arrested with Alfan. The notebook, according to his testimony, gave the names of 487 raiders and also listed their military targets and the number of raiders assigned to each operation. Photos printed from the negatives were thought to show raiders.[139]

---

[136] Human Rights Watch interview with Raider A, Ukunda, April and May, 1999.

[137] Human Rights Watch interview with Raider B, Mombasa, May 26, 1999.

[138] Michael Mumo and Ngumbao Kithi, "LSK takes up role in inquiry" *Daily Nation,* September 24, 1998. See also Akiwumi Commission Official Transcript, October 12, p. 47.

[139] Akiwumi Commission Official Transcript, October 6, 1998, pp. 44-53, 93-94, 99-101. Witnesses later identified one person shown in the photos as the raiders' commander, Bempa.

The Participation of "Outsiders"
There has been much speculation as to the origin of the well-armed, highly trained soldiers who were described as outsiders. Several reports have suggested they might have been mercenaries from Rwanda or Uganda.[140] Human Rights Watch was not able to establish the background of these men. The raiders' group clearly included Kenyans with prior military experience on whom they relied greatly, as well as some active duty members of the armed forces. The raiders, however, described one group of experienced fighters in different terms, as outsiders. In one case, a raider said that Bempa had told him the majority of the soldiers were foreigners, which he also believed to be true because of what he observed:

> There were soldiers who would come for a few days at a time (about four days) to give training, then they'd shift to somewhere else. There were about fifty of them, some from Kenya, but most were from [abroad...]. Bempa would communicate with these people and he'd arrange for them to come to do the training. These soldiers would do more rigorous training, including exercising a lot (running and jumping) and using guns. They had their own guns, but I don't know where they got them. Bempa said that when the raid happens we should follow the instructions of these soldiers, and the commanders, and that once we'd raided we too would get guns and also grenades. [...] I don't know how many of the soldiers were foreign. I just followed orders and didn't count the number to know for sure. I never spoke to them directly. I just took instructions from them. Some of the soldiers, the ones from Kenya, spoke in Swahili and the others I couldn't understand. The Kenyan soldiers would translate. Of the whole group, only a few soldiers could speak Swahili.[141]

The testimony of a second raider also supports the contention that this group was formed largely of non-locals, possibly not of Kenyan origin. Speaking separately, he described non-Swahili-speaking soldiers who would communicate orders via the local leaders; the latter could understand the soldiers, perhaps

---

[140] See, for example, KHRC, *Kayas of Deprivation,* p. 22.
[141] Human Rights Watch interview with Raider F, Mombasa, May 24, 1999.

because they were more educated and spoke English.[142]   The outsiders, as both
raiders explained, only took part in early operations and soon withdrew.

A third raider said that he had heard rumors about soldiers. He said, "We
tried to ask Swaleh [bin Alfan] about the soldiers because he'd said he had some.
He told us, 'You're not alone.' But it was a deep secret between him and the top
people."[143] He added that he had heard that "the foreigners" were at another
training site. Two raiders indicated they had never seen any outsiders and, while
they were aware of such claims, were convinced all the raiders on the South Coast
were Digos.[144] This view accorded with that of the authorities, who rejected claims
that external actors participated in the fighting.[145]

The Raider's Arsenal

The raiders' leaders placed great importance on the acquisition of firearms.
From the beginning, they had some guns at hand.[146]   The top military leader,
Bempa, always carried two pistols on his belt and the outsiders had more
sophisticated weapons. According to one raider, "[e]ach of the soldiers had his
gun. They were AK-47s and some had machine guns. One kind was shorter (about
the size of my forearm) and had a curved magazine and the other one was longer
and fired rat-tat-tat."[147] Another raider said he only saw about ten guns before the
attack, saying they were carried only by the outsiders and that "[t]he guns had a
small wooden part and a banana-shaped magazine."[148] His description is consistent
with that of several models of the Kalashnikov assault rifle, including the original
AK-47 design and various modifications to it.

But the raiders wanted more guns to enable them to carry out coordinated
attacks on up-country people, and devised ways to obtain them. One raider said:

> We needed money and arms to train people. We had to grab the
> arms from police in the Likoni area. We killed about three

---

[142] Human Rights Watch interview with Raider A, Ukunda, April 22, 1999.

[143] Human Rights Watch interview with Raider B, Mombasa, May 26, 1999.

[144] Human Rights Watch interviews with Raider B and Raider C, Coast Province, May,
1999.

[145] See, for example, Akiwumi Commission Official Transcript, October 6, 1998, p.
7.

[146] That this was the case is also clear from reports circulated to security officials,
described below.

[147] Human Rights Watch interview with Raider F, Mombasa, May 24, 1999.

[148] Human Rights Watch interview with Raider A, Ukunda, April 22, 1999.

police officers [on patrol in the area] and took their guns. We got three G3s, a pistol revolver, and an AK [Kalashnikov assault rifle]. We got the AK from another person as a contribution. He wanted to join and support the group, but he didn't. He was an ex-Air Force soldier. He didn't want to be known. [...] When we were training, someone came and dropped a box of 10,000 bullets for G3 guns. They just dropped off the box and left some G3s.[149]

Police officers confirmed that police were attacked and their weapons taken, and one said he learned that a few stolen weapons (both rifles and pistols) were in the hands of the raiders before they attacked the Likoni police station.[150]

One raider asserted that politicians supplied a few additional guns before the Likoni attack.[151] Another raider said that when they attacked Likoni, "we had been waiting for arms to come from Nairobi, but they hadn't."[152] The raiders also attempted at the time to buy guns from Somalia, one said, but were not successful.[153]

The importance of guns should not be underestimated. In the attack at Likoni, raiders armed with guns stood back and provided cover as others raided the police station and ferry police post. The same approach was used elsewhere, using the additional weapons stolen from the Likoni police station. This tactic allowed a relatively small number of raiders to wreak havoc in populated areas. The raiders' victims had little protection against such well-armed attackers. Similarly, the raiders' impressive fire power intimidated Kenyan security forces who were reluctant to pursue them. According to one of the raiders, their spiritual leader understood the difference even a few guns would make: "[Alfan] said what matters most is to acquire arms and go to the areas dominated by up-country people."[154]

---

[149] Human Rights Watch interview with Raider B, Ukunda, May 8, 1999.

[150] See, for example, Michael Mumo, "Security alert 'was ignored,'" *Daily Nation*, September 3, 1998.

[151] Human Rights Watch interview with Raider A, Ukunda, April 22, 1999. KHRC, on the evidence of a raider and a police intelligence officer, reported that some guns were supplied to the raiders by people described as Somalis. In one case, a politician was said to have made the necessary introductions. KHRC, *Kayas of Deprivation*, p. 24.

[152] Human Rights Watch interview with Raider C, Mombasa, May 9, 1999.

[153] Human Rights Watch interview with Raider B, Mombasa, May 26, 1999.

[154] Ibid.

Training

In preparation for the well-coordinated operations they would later conduct, the raiders underwent training at several sites around Coast Province. In some cases, farms that received government assistance to employ youth, called youth development projects, were used as a cover for the raiders' activities, and the raiders described using two such sites for training sessions that lasted two weeks.[155] In both locations, raiders were taught "how to shoot, how to dismantle a gun, how to clean it, how to load it" and undertook rudimentary exercises with sticks and batons.[156] The raiders said these locations were only used for training and they returned home to sleep. One of the raiders said he received rudimentary training from the local leaders, but that the outsiders provided "more rigorous training," especially in the use of guns.[157]

In addition to these training sites, one raider described a mobile camp that was used before the raids began. It was located in the Kiteje area in Kwale district. There, the raiders were issued blankets and slept in canvas tents, and the outsiders would lead them in training exercises. The raider who said he was based at this camp explained that, although he did not visit any other training sites, the group leaders made a point to say that young men elsewhere were also preparing for the raids.[158]

The Raiders Strike

The Likoni Attack

The organizers of the raids had been carefully preparing for months to carry out violent attacks and, when the raids began on August 13, many assumed that date had been selected in advance by the group leaders. The group leaders, according to the raiders, kept secret the date of the planned attack, but the violence was sparked earlier than intended after they grew worried that some of their

---

[155] Human Rights Watch interviews with Raider A and Raider B, Coast Province, April and May 1999.

[156] Human Rights Watch interview with Raider B, Ukunda, May 8, 1999; Human Rights Watch interview with Raider F, Mombasa, May 24, 1999.

[157] Human Rights Watch interview with Raider F, Mombasa, May 24, 1999.

[158] Human Rights Watch interview with Raider A, Ukunda, April 22, 1999, and Mombasa, May 21, 1999.

associates had been arrested and ordered the raiders to act.[159]   One raider said Alfan gave the order to start the raids.[160]

Raiders who participated in the Likoni attack described an operation executed with military precision.[161]   On the evening of August 13, the group leaders sent word to their recruits to prepare for an attack at 8:30 that night. The order went out by 4 p.m., and by 7 p.m. the raiders left their home areas for Likoni. According to one raider who was there that night, a politician sent a lorry that was used to transport the group leaders and outsiders, together with some of the raiders, to the outskirts of Likoni. From there they continued on foot. Another raider said he arrived on foot with others.

Once in Likoni, the raiders were divided into two groups, with one group instructed to go to the police station and the other sent to the ferry police post. These were the bases for local security personnel who could have interfered with the raiders' attacks on up-country residents. Moreover, the police station housed a store of needed firearms, and the ferry was of strategic importance as the transportation link to Mombasa island, where further security personnel were based. The raiders clearly felt animosity toward the police, whom they viewed as up-country-dominated and highly abusive of their community, and this presumably also contributed to the selection of their initial target.

Following orders, the raiders waited until 8:30 p.m. to launch a simultaneous attack. In both locations, the raiders carrying guns stayed at a distance while the others, armed with hidden knives and other traditional weapons, approached the police. As one raider explained, "When we raided Likoni, those with the guns (the soldiers) weren't in the front lines. We pretended like we were bringing someone [a thief] in to be arrested and then we attacked and got the guns."[162] Police officials have confirmed that the raiders stole forty-three G3 rifles that night, along with a handful of other firearms and approximately 1,500 rounds of ammunition.[163]

At the police station in particular, the raid was executed with planning and coordination. A raider who was there said twenty-seven men took part in the operation.[164] He explained that the attackers were divided into smaller groups, with

---

[159] Human Rights Watch interviews with Raider A and Raider B, Coast Province, April and May 1999.

[160] Human Rights Watch interview with Raider B, Ukunda, May 8, 1999.

[161] Human Rights Watch interviews with Raider A, Ukunda, April 22, 1999; Raider B, Ukunda, May 8, 1999; and Raider F, Mombasa, May 24, 1999.

[162] Human Rights Watch interview with Raider F, Mombasa, May 24, 1999.

[163] Njihia and Kimemia, "Raiders 'took....,'" *Daily Nation.*

[164] Human Rights Watch interview with Raider B, Ukunda, May 8, 1999.

ten raiders sent to the area chief's nearby office, ten deployed to surround the fence outside, and seven sent inside the police station. Those who entered the station attacked the police with machetes and bows and arrows. Using these traditional weapons, they killed three police officers. They also released all the prisoners in jail, stole a police radio (in addition to robbing the armory), and proceeded to set fire to the police station, adjacent administration offices, and nearby homes. When some police officers tried to shoot at them, the raiders with guns returned fire. At the ferry police post, the raiders used a similar approach. They surrounded and killed two policemen while others stood back holding guns and also killed another police officer as they left the area. A police officer who survived the attack stated, "The raiders wanted to acquire firearms and to disable us in order to carry out their mission."[165] Police witnesses said they only saw their attackers wield bows and arrows and other traditional weapons.[166]

Next, the raiders went on an all-night rampage around Likoni. A raider said, "After we got the guns, we went and attacked the non-local people—killing, burning, chasing people."[167] He indicated that they targeted people from up-country, going house by house. They checked to see if someone was Digo by calling out a greeting and waiting to see if they answered in the Digo language. They brutally attacked and maimed their victims using machetes and other crude instruments. One raider defected later that night because he was disturbed by the violence, saying: "People did things at Likoni that I did not agree with. They entered people's houses and killed people in cold blood."[168]

Throughout the night the raiders carried out attacks, including burning local administration buildings and market kiosks largely operated by up-country vendors, without interference from security forces. As one raider put it, "We dominated the area for eight hours until the morning."[169] The response by the government's security forces was slow and ineffectual. On the night of the Likoni raid, police and paramilitary units of the General Service Unit (GSU) were very slow to appear at the scene. When security forces finally began to appear on the morning of August 14, the raiders withdrew into hiding places on the South Coast,

---

[165] Michael Mumo, "Ex-Army men 'led Likoni attack,'" *Daily Nation,* September 4, 1998.

[166] Unofficial transcript of police testimony presented in the criminal case against suspected raiders, provided by a lawyer for the defense, copy on file with Human Rights Watch.

[167] Human Rights Watch interview with Raider C, Mombasa, May 9, 1999.

[168] Human Rights Watch interview with Raider A, Mombasa, May 21, 1999.

[169] Human Rights Watch interview with Raider B, Ukunda, May 8, 1999.

particularly the Kaya Bombo forest and the Similani caves. (For this reason, they became known as the Kaya Bombo raiders.) In addition to the six slain police officers, the raiders killed at least six other people that evening and various others were maimed or otherwise injured. In a brutal pattern that was repeated for weeks, most of the casualties were victims of multiple wounds caused by machetes or knives.

The Raiders Regroup

Other than sporadic firefights with government security forces, who mostly avoided encounters with the well-armed raiders, little stood in the way of the raiders. To the contrary, the virtual security vacuum in the wake of the Likoni attack, described in full below, permitted them to regroup in order to carry out further well-organized attacks. Of the estimated two hundred people who had participated in the August 13 attack at Likoni, only seventy-three remained, according to one raider, and their composition changed significantly. The soldiers whom some raiders had described as outsiders withdrew and were not involved in subsequent attacks. Apparently they had fulfilled their purpose. As one raider explained, "We now had weapons so we didn't need the soldiers, and we'd be sent out on raids without them."[170]

The raiders added and trained new recruits. As one put it, "We were fighting with the GSU and training our men at the same time."[171] The new recruits were mostly sympathizers and hangers-on, however, rather than experienced fighters. One raider decided to join the day following the Likoni raid when a group of some forty armed raiders passed through his area on its way to the Kaya Bombo forest. He explained that young boys aged twelve to seventeen years old attempted to join as well but were sent home.[172] Another raider pointed out that some active-duty military men from navy and army barracks joined them. He said, "When the government called in the army, some Mijikenda helped us and gave arms or ran away [deserted or took unauthorized leave] from the army."[173]

The raiders conceived a uniform and had twenty-four of them made to be worn during the attacks. As described by several raiders and witnesses, the uniform consisted of a black cape or robe with two bands of fabric, one red and one

---

[170] Human Rights Watch interview with Raider F, Mombasa, May 24, 1999. As the raids progressed, they became increasingly disorganized. KHRC, *Kayas of Deprivation*, pp. 35-36.

[171] Human Rights Watch interview with Raider C, Mombasa, May 9, 1999.

[172] Human Rights Watch interview with Raider D, Mombasa, May 9, 1999.

[173] Human Rights Watch interview with Raider B, Ukunda, May 8, 1999.

white, crossing the chest in an "X" pattern and also featured a star and crescent moon at the front and, at least in some cases, the Islamic saying "There is No God but Allah" (symbolizing the mix of Muslim and animist faith among the Digo raiders). These uniforms were generally worn by the more prominent raiders, particularly those Digos who had significant military experience. As explained by one raider, they were believed to afford special protection: "When you are led by people wearing these robes, you cannot be seen by your enemy and you are protected by the spirits."[174] While witnesses also reported that the raiders wore shorts and red headbands and, some said, camouflage, the raiders themselves only spoke of wearing the black robe or street clothes with a hood to hide their faces and did not clarify whether the servicemen among their ranks might have worn camouflage. They also told of painting slogans and distributing leaflets threatening up-country residents. One widely-circulated leaflet read, "The time has come for us original inhabitants of the coast to claim what is rightly ours. We must remove these invaders from our land."[175]

The Raids Continue

The raiders launched further raids from the hideouts that served as their new base of operations. These included attacks in several area towns and villages in mid-August that added to the mounting death toll. The attackers in front invariably carried firearms, making the slaughter possible. The raiders who spoke to Human Rights Watch participated in these raids, as well as attacks into September in which they killed and maimed further victims. Several attacks took place in or near Ukunda, most notably two attacks in resort areas: a September 5 attack at Shelly Beach and a September 11 raid on Ukunda that ended with a firefight at Diani Beach.

A witness described the September 11 raid at Ukunda, which had begun with an attack on the police station, in which the raiders quickly overpowered police:

> I saw a large crowd of people coming from the direction of the police station toward the post office; some of them were running, and I heard gunshots from the direction of the police station, as if there was an exchange of fire. Then everyone was running, including old men, women, and children. These were the first gunshots I have heard in the entire period that I have

---

[174] Human Rights Watch interview with Raider C, Mombasa, May 9, 1999.
[175] Human Rights Watch, *Human Right Watch World Report 1998* (New York: Human Rights Watch, 1997), p. 42.

lived in this area. [My friend] said: "These are the raiders from
the Kaya Bombo. Let's run!" At first I didn't believe him. [...]
We heard people shouting: "They're coming on the old road!"
so I went to check it out.[176]

There were some fifty raiders, he said, some of them wearing the robe
uniform, and the way they walked made clear they had had military training:

They were taking proper cover. Some in the front were carrying
guns, about eleven guys. They were covering each other,
holding their guns up and firing in the air. They were AKs. I
know these guns. I used to handle them when I was in the
military. (The police have G3s.) There was a commander
among them who was carrying a radio in one hand and a stick in
the other (the stick is about one meter long and is used by police
and army officers); I did not see if he had a gun.[177]

As the raiders came closer, he saw that the men behind the first group of
raiders were carrying machetes and bows and arrows, waving to onlookers and
looting the kiosks along the road. These men were followed by some local women
and children, who danced in apparent celebration. The commander called out in
Swahili to local Digo residents, telling them they were not in danger and should
feel free to take part in the looting of the kiosks. Once the raiders reached the
center of town, the raid turned violent. The commander, pointing at certain
businesses with his stick, began instructing his men to burn them down, which they
did. At about the same time, the raiders opened fire on the post office, where some
residents were hiding. As the crowd ran from the raiders, the witness's friend was
shot and fell dead. From a distance, the witness saw the raiders proceed south
down the main road, moving slowly and burning kiosks along the way. He said he
later learned that the security forces arrived about an hour after the raiders first
appeared in Ukunda, and fifteen minutes after they had left the area.[178]
      The vast majority of attacks, particularly well-organized ones, were
concentrated in the Likoni-Kwale area. These were also the most brutal attacks,

---

[176] Human Rights Watch interview with an eyewitness, Ukunda, April 21, 1999.
[177] Ibid.
[178] Ibid. Government security forces were reported to have engaged in an extended
firefight with the raiders at Diani after reinforcements arrived. "New Attacks in Mombasa,"
Daily Nation, September 12, 1997.

often resulting in deaths or seriously injured by gruesome means. Many victims, once identified as up-country residents from their identity cards or because they did not speak the Digo language, were repeatedly stabbed with knives, slashed with machetes, or otherwise maimed. Residents of the area expressed shock at the brutality of the attacks, given that the area had previously been peaceful and that the different ethnic communities had lived together in relative harmony for generations.[179]

The raiders also said they killed several police officers during operations and took their guns. While some raiders remained active with the force for weeks, those interviewed disavowed attacks that primarily involved looting as well as the burning of market kiosks in an August 19 incident in Malindi, on the North Coast. They attributed such attacks instead to disaffected local people who took advantage of the confusion, lax security, and heightened ethnic tensions to settle scores or rob their neighbors. They did not touch on the subject of sexual violence, in particular allegations of rape of up-country women by raiders, which surfaced mostly in the later phases of the violence.[180]

Response of the Security Forces: Complicity or Incompetence?

The raiders, from the time they began organizing for violence until long after they attacked the Likoni police station, were able to operate in a virtual security vacuum. No efforts were made to stop the raiders before the raids were launched, despite numerous advance warnings. Once the violence began, government security forces—inclusive of the police, paramilitary GSU, and army and navy troops—did not mount serious security operations directed against the raiders and instead took a number of steps that undermined their effective pursuit. In addition, they failed to provide adequate protection to the victims of the targeted raids and were responsible for a number of serious human rights abuses, including arbitrary arrests and torture. The response of the government's security forces to the violence was so lax as to raise widespread suspicions of government complicity in the attacks.

Turning a Blind Eye

As the raiders on the South Coast were preparing for their first attack, numerous Kenyan authorities at different levels were informed of serious security problems and failed to take action. As concluded in a mid-September 1997 police report on the violence, prepared by the deputy director of the Criminal

---

[179] KHRC, *Kayas of Deprivation*, p. 31.
[180] KHRC, *Kayas of Deprivation*, pp. 34-35; KHRC, *Abandoned to Terror.*

Investigations Department following a visit to Coast Province: "It is apparent that the initial launching of the clashes and period it started was known to the security agencies within the area."[181] Authorities in Nairobi were also warned of security threats in the area.

The fact that government officials had been forewarned and failed to act on the information became public knowledge largely because of the efforts of a private citizen, Roshanali Karmali Pradhan (known as "Jimmy"). Prior to the August raid Pradhan repeatedly informed authorities at the local, district, and provincial level in writing about suspicious activities conducted by groups of young men on his farm near the Likoni-Kwale border. After a May 15, 1997, letter to the local chief, copied to a number of area security officials, went unanswered, Prahdan wrote to the Likoni police chief on August 4 stating that, "a gang of 15-20 men have made a base at one boundary of my farm lying on the Mombasa Kwale boundary. These men are armed with guns and other weapons. [...] They gather there every Friday and terrorsies [sic] the area over the weekend." Again, the letter was copied to other security and administration officials. Those to whom at least one of Pradhan's letters were addressed or copied included the provincial commissioner (PC), the provincial police officer (PPO), the provincial criminal investigations officer (PCIO), the district commissioner (DC) of Kwale, the district officer (DO) of Matuga, the heads of the three police stations (Likoni, Kwale, and Diani), and the chief of his area.[182]

The information supplied by Pradhan was later supplemented by the testimony to the Akiwumi Commission of several police officials, ranging from local to provincial level and particularly intelligence officials, who made clear that they were aware of oathing and training activities in the Likoni-Kwale area months before the August 13 raid. For example, the most senior intelligence official at the provincial level (the provincial security intelligence officer or PSIO) testified that as early as May 1997 he received reports that a large group of young men had stolen several guns from police and were planning to disrupt the elections in order to bring majimbo to the Coast region. One report predicted an attack by hundreds

---

[181] "A Report on Ethnic Clashes in Coast Province-Likoni and the Surrounding Areas," Criminal Investigations Department (Kenyan police), undated but from late September 1997, signed by the deputy CID director (hereafter "Police Report-Likoni"), copy on file with Human Rights Watch, p. 8. In testimony before the Akiwumi Commission, the report's author sought to distance himself from this conclusion. Akiwumi Commission Official Transcript, July 22, 1998, p. 27.

[182] Letters from Roshanali Karmali Pradhan to various security officials, presented as evidence to the Akiwumi Commission, copies on file with Human Rights Watch.

of Digo youths on the Likoni police station and the homes of up-country residents. The specific date given for that attack (May 18, 1997) ultimately proved incorrect, but later intelligence reports included a new warning in July 1997, less than a month before the August 1997 attack, that the Likoni police station would be burned down, as well as information that the group of youths included many active-duty and former servicemen. Despite having all this information at hand, the PSIO's provincial security counterparts said he never shared it with them, contradicting his testimony. Instead, over the months prior to the attack the PSIO's only confirmed action was to notify his superiors in Nairobi and order further investigations from his subordinates, and he said he also instructed police stations to be on alert. He claimed there was nothing else he could do since "it was not known when the attack would take place."[183]

One case from Kwale helps illustrate the complacency exhibited. The district criminal investigations officer (DCIO), already aware of reports that Muslim youths and ex-servicemen intended to take part in forthcoming attacks on police targets to steal weapons and ammunition, investigated claims that a local acrobatic troupe had undergone military training in Uganda. His mid-July report to the PCIO read in part: "The troupe would evidently be part of the trained Mercenaries earmarked for [that] job."[184] Despite earlier reports to him by a different officer about plans to use violence to drive away up-country people, the PCIO opted to leave the matter of the training in the hands of junior intelligence personnel, who were to conduct further inquiries.[185]

The director of Kenya's National Security Intelligence Service (previously known as the Security Intelligence Department) at the time testified before the Akiwumi Commission that from about May 1997 he was informed of security threats in Coast Province, which were conveyed to him by his juniors via standard reporting channels. He noted that he informed the Police Commissioner, as well as the top government official responsible for internal security, by phone, of the

---

[183] Akiwumi Commission Official Transcript, October 8, 1998, p. 59-73; Mugasia, "Raid suspect held"; Njeri Rugene, "Security men told of conflict," *Daily Nation*, May 27, 1999.

[184] "Security Intelligence: Jambo Mambo International Acrobats Troupe," submitted by the DCIO Kwale to the PCIO Coast Province, dated July 21, 1997, copy on file with Human Rights Watch.

[185] Akiwumi Commission Official Transcript, October 7, 1998, pp. 8-11, 27-28; Akiwumi Commission Official Transcript, October 8, 1998, p. 70; Noel Mwakugu, "Acrobats 'joined former soldiers before attacks,'" *East African Standard*, September 12, 1998.

reports from Coast Province, but that the matter was still under investigation when the raiders struck on August 13, 1997.[186] Thus the widely diffused warnings about upcoming attacks in Coast Province did not lead to effective action to prevent the raids. The Likoni police station chief, who allegedly had been informed of the threat against his station, took no extra precautions and no additional personnel were deployed. He also left early the day of the attack, raising further suspicions. In one of only a handful of disciplinary actions following the Likoni raid, the station chief was transferred and later dismissed from the police force for negligence and disobeying orders.[187]

Various officials testified that their colleagues who had been forewarned did not inform them of reports of impending violence, and suspicions that some officials may have sought to conceal what they knew came to the fore during police investigations launched after the raid. In several cases, police witnesses charged that others had engaged in a cover-up. The police officer sent from Nairobi to investigate the clashes gave an example of the deception, saying top Coast Province security officials acted to keep from him information about advance warnings, such as the letters from Jimmy Pradhan which they had disregarded. This officer was reassigned and taken off the case, and his team, under the direction of a new provincial criminal investigations chief, took over the investigation.[188]

The September 1997 police report concluded: "[T]he Provincial Administration, the Police, as well as the Security Intelligence had this vital information well in advance but failed to co-ordinate and act upon it in good time as was expected."[189] The raiders said police inaction made it possible for them to conduct their planning in peace. One said: "We had to keep our activities secret. Messages were sent to senior police [by others], but they took no action. [...] No one came and disturbed us at all."[190]

---

[186] Akiwumi Commission Official Transcript, May 28, 1999, pp. 87-91.

[187] See, for example, Njeri Rugene, "'We lacked funds to combat violence'- ex-police boss," *Daily Nation*, June 4, 1999. In failing to take any action, he apparently ignored a general order from Nairobi that all police stations be placed on alert in anticipation of the upcoming elections, as well as the order the PSIO said he gave. The former Likoni police chief, who asserted that he was removed from his position rather than formally dismissed, denied the claims against him. Akiwumi Commission Official Transcript, October 2, 1998, pp. 1-9, 44-56.

[188] See, for example, Michael Mumo and Patrick Mayoyo, "Move to derail probe alleged," *Daily Nation*, September 8, 1998; Rugene, "Security men told of conflict."

[189] "Police Report-Likoni," p. 9.

[190] Human Rights Watch interview with Raider B, Ukunda, May 8, 1999.

Inaction Against Perpetrators

From the time the Likoni raid was launched on August 13, and for weeks thereafter, the government's poor security response made the deadly chaos possible. On the night of the first raid at the Likoni police station, personnel at a Kenyan Navy base located two kilometers from the scene of the raiders' attack did not respond, although the shots would have been audible. GSU units and police reinforcements arrived at Likoni by ferry from Mombasa several hours after the raiders attacked the police station and police post. They said they were unable to cross for hours because raiders shot at the ferry.[191]

The Kenyan military was briefly called to assist in the security operation, but army and navy personnel were both withdrawn within a matter of a few days. Officials stated that they involved the military in the operation at first because they believed the violence was perpetrated by an external force from another country but called them off when they decided that it was an internal matter.[192]

Accounts of skirmishes between security forces and the raiders indicate that they were well-matched or that the raiders may have had a military advantage. This demonstrates both the preparation and coordination of the raiders, but also the dismal failings of the state security operation. In one early case, a group of ten policemen was making its way to join up with other security forces in the Kaya Bombo forest area when a group of raiders appeared and the police commander, at the sight of them, ran away leaving his men behind, later claiming that his forces were outnumbered and outgunned. In another instance, officials testified that security forces totaling fifty men, including a platoon of thirty-five army soldiers and operating under army command, engaged the raiders in a heavy exchange of gunfire, but were overpowered and were forced to withdraw. Apparently describing the same incident, officials testified that reinforcements were not deployed because it was late afternoon and the army did not want to risk fighting at night. Similarly, a raider told how raiders and GSU personnel engaged in an

---

[191] "Police went to Likoni 'too late,'" *Daily Nation*, August 18, 1998; Mumo,"Ex-Army men...," *Daily Nation*.

[192] Amadi Mugasia, "Raid thought to be external," *East African Standard*, October 7, 1998.

armed skirmish outside Kaya Bombo forest until "the GSU finally got scared and left."[193]

The ineptitude of the security response immediately following the Likoni raid might be attributed to the confusion of the early days, but this pattern persisted even when the security operation was in full swing, leading to suspicions that the failings of the security forces were deliberate. When security forces came across the raiders, they often failed to engage them, chose not to pursue them as the raiders escaped, and even fled themselves to avoid an armed confrontation. For example, Jimmy Pradhan was at his farm with a government security escort when they saw a group of armed raiders at one end of his farm. Together with security forces who were patrolling the area, there were more than thirty fully armed security men, he said, but the GSU commander rejected requests to order an immediate attack and instead called for a helicopter, which took an hour to arrive, to follow the raiders. "[N]o attempt was made to apprehend or engage them," Pradhan stated.[194]

The raiders themselves indicated that they could easily hide from the security forces and, when they were discovered, scare them off by firing at them, and some became suspicious of the government's security operation. One stated:

> If the government would have wanted to destroy us they could have done it because they have so much power. We wondered how the government was performing their [sic] duty because we'd see the people come and then they'd go away. We don't know who was ordering this. If they'd been told we'd taken this route, they'd take another. At first, they brought the Kenyan Army and everybody to fight us but later they learned the situation and just let us be. [...] We don't know why they didn't come after us. But later I came to realize that we were used for

---

[193] Human Rights Watch interview with Raider D, Mombasa, May 9, 1999; Ngumbao Kithi and Michael Mumo, "Why I abandoned my men in Likoni—Commander," *Daily Nation*, September 27, 1998; "Two APs were killed in fight with raiders, witness claims," *East African Standard*, September 23, 1998; Akiwumi Commission Official Transcript, October 15, 1998, p. 129-30.

[194] Letter dated August 13, 1998, from Roshanali Karmali Pradhan, copy on file with Human Rights Watch; Akiwumi Commission Official Transcript, August 25, 1998, pp. 48-51.

political reasons. I realized this was being planned during [voter] registration.[195]

In addition, a number of top Coast Province security personnel were suddenly replaced in September, in the middle of the security operation, and these sudden changes further impeded efforts to halt the raiders. The raiders also noticed the difference:

> [T]he head [security] people were transferred immediately after the attack and that really helped us. The new people didn't know their way around. They sent new people from remote places. We took advantage of this. [...] After the Intelligence body was transferred, everything changed. Even us, we wondered why these people instead of coming to us went to attack innocent people, not coming to where we were.[196]

The raider speculated that the raiders' political contacts had arranged this change on their behalf.

Several police officials indicated that transportation and communication difficulties in the early days, as well as a lack of reinforcements and lack of cooperation from local administration officials, presented difficulties. Others, however, pointed to more serious problems, saying their operations were poorly managed and suffered from "a disjointed command and lack of proper coordination," as well as in-fighting among members of the provincial security committee (PSC), and that security forces failed to act on timely tips about where the raiders and the stolen guns could be found.[197]

Then-provincial police chief Francis Gichuki was singled out for blame by several of his former colleagues, who accused him of acting to undermine the government security operations. Officials testified, for example, that he blocked joint operations, redirected police forces to less important areas, transferred personnel, and refused to cooperate with other top security officials. When Gichuki was suddenly transferred in September 1997 without public explanation, as were other members of his team, some observers stated it was because he had

---

[195] Human Rights Watch interview with Raider B, Mombasa, May 26, 1999.
[196] Ibid.
[197] Patrick Mayoyo and Michael Mumo, "Judges say reluctant Maitha must testify," *Daily Nation*, October 6, 1998; Amadi Mugasia, "Police differed over clashes," *East African Standard*, September 9, 1998.

been slow to act, while Gichuki's defenders argued that he was replaced as PPO in retaliation for the arrest of prominent ruling party politicians.[198]

Gichuki was keenly aware of a political dimension to the violence. One official testified that the PPO told him, "The whole issue regarding the raiders is political and I do not want to be involved."[199] Gichuki himself testified that he came to strongly believe that the violence was politically motivated. He complained in particular of extensive political interference in security operations, described below. He stated that he had a great deal of information on the violence, but would only provide it if a closed session were to be arranged:

> [There] are some names I cannot give in public. Whatever you say here appears in the newspapers the following morning. The people in Nairobi know me and they will say that I told you everything. I am an ex-Government servant and I cannot say everything here. I have been in the system. This is a political government and I cannot come saying everything here. Some of the things are confidential.[200]

Lack of Protection for the Victims

The government's failure to mount an adequate security response meant the up-country people forced to flee by the violence were unable to return. Human rights groups estimated that the violence, in which at least one hundred people were killed, also resulted in the displacement of over 100,000 people. Up to four thousand sought refuge in the Likoni Catholic Church, but police protection there was inadequate, despite requests for greater security, and armed raiders attacked the church compound on August 22, killing two people. Moreover, schools had to be closed due to persistent insecurity and lack of police protection.[201]

---

[198] See, for example, Akiwumi Commission Official Transcript, October 6, 1998, pp. 9-16; Mayoyo and Mumo, "Judges say...," *Daily Nation*; KHRC, *Kayas of Deprivation*, p. 40.

[199] Michael Mumo and Ngumbao Kithi, "Likoni: Officer says police were divided," *Daily Nation*, September 10, 1998.

[200] Akiwumi Commission Official Transcript, October 15, 1998, pp. 14-15. See also Patrick Mayoyo and Michael Mumo, "Ex-police boss seeks to testify in camera," *Daily Nation*, October 16, 1998.

[201] KHRC, *Kayas Revisited*, p. 32; African Rights (London), "Violence at the Coast: The Human Consequences of Kenya's Crumbling Political Institutions," *Witness*, Issue 2, October-November 1997, pp. 2, 6-8; "Poor turnout at schools," *Daily Nation*, September 9, 1997.

Furthermore, security forces failed to deploy to areas where the raiders had struck and some areas, including Likoni itself, were subsequently the subject of repeated attacks and looting. For example, raiders armed with at least one gun attacked the farm owned by Jimmy Pradhan on August 14, killing an up-country employee, causing extensive property damage, and stealing some farm animals. Pradhan made repeated requests for police action over the course of several months, which were not met. He later filed a lawsuit against the Kenyan government for damages resulting from this raid and continued looting that police forces failed to prevent—even, as noted above, when they witnessed the raiders on his property.[202]

After almost a month of confusion and inaction following the Likoni raid, the government announced that it had prepared a security plan to halt the violence and protect civilians. Operation orders issued in mid-September show that security forces at that point totaled 1,080 people, including police personnel from throughout the area, paramilitary forces, members of specialized security units, and others.[203] (The government never lived up to an early promise to deploy 20,000 security personnel to quell the violence.)

It was not until several weeks later, however, that the government began to flush out the raiders from their hideouts. In a security operation in early November, the police ousted raiders from a den in the Similani caves, reported to have housed as many as thirty—but made no arrests. According to police announcements, the government recovered a few rifles and a submachine-gun, ammunition, a large tent, some of the raiders' uniforms, and their logbook, among other items. The new PPO, in place since September, distinguished this operation from previous ones, stating: "[This operation] will continue until we flush out all the raiders. This time we will not stop until we end this menace."[204]

The long delay in organizing and mounting a serious security operation is striking, and even the November 1997 operation—billed as the government's most effective action and attributed to the arrival of needed reinforcements—did not result in the capture of the raiders or an end to their activities. To the contrary,

---

[202] Human Rights Watch interview with R.K. ("Jimmy") Pradhan, April 20, 1999, Mombasa; Civil Suit no. 276 of 1998, filed in the High Court of Kenya at Mombasa; Akiwumi Commission Official Transcript, August 27, 1998, pp. 12-21. In his lawsuit, Pradhan alleges negligence and breach of duty and demands civil damages.

[203] Provincial Police Headquarters, "Operation Orders 'Operation Taputa Mnaz,'" September 17, 1997, copy on file with Human Rights Watch, pp. 6-7.

[204] Edmund Kwela and Patrick Mayoyo, "Raiders evicted from caves," *Daily Nation*, November 2, 1997; Njihia and Kimemia, "Raiders 'took...,'" *Daily Nation*.

sporadic raids continued well into November—although they increasingly took the form of banditry. A small band of raiders defied police for more than a year after that, continuing to conduct armed robberies in the area and even promoting their activities with a broadcast on BBC radio in Kenya, until a December 1998 police ambush in which Bempa and several of the raiders' remaining military leaders were killed.

Torture and Ill-Treatment

The Kenyan security forces were responsible for an indiscriminate crackdown on the Digo population of the South Coast after the initial raids, even while largely avoiding confrontation with the raiders themselves. Human Rights Watch heard numerous first-hand testimonies of widespread and serious human rights abuses. Patterns of excessive use of force by security forces, police brutality, and torture in Kenya have been well documented and are not specific to the Coast region. In this case, the interviewees described being beaten, tortured, and severely mistreated during detention. The violations took place following the killing of several police officers in the Likoni attack, when the detainees were picked up in security sweeps of mostly Digo youths.

Security forces, while avoiding confrontations with the armed raiders at their hideouts, undertook security operations that targeted residents of coastal villages and towns. As one raider put it, "They chased the Digos for revenge. Instead of looking for us, they killed innocent people."[205] Human rights groups documented that the officially sanctioned sweeps, involving combined units of GSU, police, and other security personnel, resulted in indiscriminate arrests of hundreds of mostly Digo men, widespread incidents of rape, and systematic looting.[206]

Those detained by the police were severely mistreated. A Digo man who claimed he had not been involved in the raids said he suffered repeated abuse after he was picked up by police. He was transported, handcuffed and lying face down, in the back of a pickup truck. The metal burned him, he said, but when he attempted to move, "the police would hit my buttocks and legs and head with their gun butts." He was taken to a police station, where the beatings continued. He explained:

> Over there they started beating me while asking "How many people did you kill?" "Where are your people?" "We know you

---

[205] Human Rights Watch interview with Raider B, Mombasa, May 26, 1999.

[206] KHRC, *Kayas of Deprivation*, pp. 42-44; African Rights, "Violence at the Coast," pp. 18-19; KHRC, *Abandoned to Terror*, pp. 8-13.

trained them." I was ordered to stand with my hands on the floor and my feet against the wall upside down and told to count to 1,000. When I fell over after a while, seven police beat me with hose pipes on the back of my neck.[207]

A raider who was captured with a friend after defecting from the group had a similar experience. He said: "We were beaten very badly by the police in Diani police station for two days. We were just being beaten and told that we had participated in the raid on the Likoni police station. We were not asked any questions."[208] Swaleh bin Alfan likewise complained of mistreatment by the police, whom he said beat him and stole cash and valuables when they came to his house to arrest him for illegal oathing and other crimes associated with the violence.[209]

Digos were the primary civilian victims of government forces charged with pursuing the raiders, but they were not alone. Individuals near the scene of the Likoni police station raid were also targeted without regard to their presumed guilt or innocence. An up-country man who happened to be driving in the Likoni ferry area on the night of the raid described how he and others were brutalized by security forces who apparently were seeking revenge—and included innocent people among the targets:

> The police were saying, "Let's kill these men, they killed the askaris [police]." One jumped on me with his boots on and broke my rib. [...] The GSU guy was hitting me with the muzzle of the gun to hurt my kidney. [...] They were whooping war cries and beating us at the same time. People came out [from hiding] to get protection from the police. [...] The police lined them up on the ground and started beating them, men and women both. They said horrible things in Swahili to one girl. The GSUs called them guerrillas. They said I was transporting guerrillas. [...] The police forced us to crawl on our hands and knees toward the ferry and were beating us, kicking us with boots. [...] It was fun for them to walk on us.[210]

---

[207] Human Rights Watch interview with a former detainee, Mombasa, May 10, 1999.
[208] Human Rights Watch interview with Raider A, Ukunda, April 22, 1999.
[209] Human Rights Watch interview with Swaleh bin Alfan, Denyenye, May 25, 1999.
[210] Human Rights Watch interview with an up-country man, Mombasa, April 23, 1999.

The group crossed the ferry, still on its knees, and was loaded into a lorry that was taken to the central police station:

> I was so glad when I saw where I was because I realized they planned to arrest us, not kill us. [...] The cells have lots of bugs and no room. To harass us, the police would tell all of us to get in the cells. [...] They know you can't fit. They just want to be cruel and exercise authority. They'd come and kick me even though I was hurt.[211]

Other detainees agreed that the overcrowding and poor prison conditions were a serious problem. One raider described the situation:

> The conditions at Central Police Station were awful. People had no food. Some even drank their own urine. The lucky ones have cells on the sides, but most of us were crowded into the central courtyard with no food and water and a bad stench.[212]

Another raider stated:

> One colleague was cut with a panga [machete] on the head and got infected with insects. He didn't get any medical attention and he died. [...] The following morning, after my colleague's death, I was taken back [to the police station]. We were forced to squat naked for twelve hours, lined up in about three rows. One officer recorded our names and then they'd call us [to be released].[213]

Moreover, a number of detainees held in connection with the raids reported torture by the police. Sixteen suspects filed a lawsuit against the government alleging serious injuries as the result of the application of a corrosive substance to their genitals, which they claimed had been ordered by prison authorities. An independent medical assessment concluded that the substance, which was

---

[211] Ibid.

[212] Human Rights Watch interview with a former detainee, Mombasa, May 10, 1999.

[213] Human Rights Watch interview with Raider F, Mombasa, May 24, 1999.

purported to be an antiseptic or antifungal agent, could have made them impotent or infertile.[214]

Former detainees interviewed independently gave Human Rights Watch testimonies that were consistent.   They described being taken to a large interrogation chamber that was outfitted with two tables. There, they were told to remove their clothes and wait on their knees as others were tortured, until it was their turn. One detainee, a Digo man who had already suffered extensive police beatings, described the torture method:

> [They] made me crouch down, put a wooden stick behind my bent knees, wrapped my arms under the stick, and then tied my hands together at my knees so I couldn't move. Then they picked me up and balanced the stick between both tables. Because of my weight, I immediately was upside down, tied onto this stick. Then they proceeded to beat me. Sometimes one of them, sometimes more. They had flat wooden planks. They were saying, "You don't want to tell us what happened?" [...] They beat the soles of my feet until they blistered and also my legs and buttocks. After that they released me and made me jump like a frog on my blistered feet hundreds of times. The room was full of about thirty other people [detainees] at different stages of this torture. They were also tying a string around people's testicles, pulling it tight and then leading them around the room like that. They were going through all of us one by one.[215]

Another person, a captured raider, described being subjected to the same torture:

> At the police headquarters, I was tied at the elbows and knees around a stick and then suspended upside down between two tables and hit on the feet, knees, and arms. Five policemen hit me one after another until they were all tired. After being beaten, a nylon string was tied twice around my testicles and then I was pulled around the room twice. The room was a big hall with two other rooms attached. I could not see others but I

---

[214] See, for example, "Suspects want to be paid for injuries," *Daily Nation*, August 25, 1998.

[215] Human Rights Watch interview with a former detainee, Mombasa, May 10, 1999.

could hear them screaming. The room is on the ground floor overlooking the sea, but there is no window. I was asked where the guns were and who was behind these attacks. I said I didn't know. They beat me five times, each time for about one hour.[216]

A third victim told the same story:

A police officer with a gap in his teeth took me to a room with a table on each side. I was tortured there. I was tied with my hands and my feet tied together and hung upside down between the two tables and a baton was place on the back of my knees. I was beaten on the soles of the feet. The police office asked what I knew about killing police, burning houses, and stealing guns. They said they'd kill me and I refused to give any names. After beating my feet, they'd tell me to jog. My feet still hurt. I have aches in the morning and at night. They also tied my genitals with a rope and pulled. This treatment lasted about one week.[217]

This individual, who was also a captured raider, still had heavily scarred feet two years later.

One of the raiders noted that since the torture:

I have problems with my groin and the joints in my arms. I cannot sleep with my wife any more. I can't work as a driver any more because I cannot grip the steering wheel. I saw a doctor but he wanted me to get an X-ray and I could not afford it, so I have not gotten any medical treatment.[218]

Some of those who gave testimony of torture were raiders who had been picked up in the indiscriminate sweeps conducted by the Kenyan security forces. The raiders with whom Human Rights Watch spoke were not convicted for their involvement in the raids. Three of them were detained but, as noted below, only one of those was prosecuted, in a criminal trial of 240 accused raiders that ultimately resulted in acquittal. Few politicians who were implicated in the violence were charged and in only a few instances did the cases go to trial (see below).

---

[216] Human Rights Watch interview with Raider C, Mombasa, May 9, 1999.
[217] Human Rights Watch interview with Raider F, Mombasa, May 24, 1999.
[218] Human Rights Watch interview with Raider C, Mombasa, May 9, 1999.

KANU's Political Maneuvers Aid the Raiders

The evidence strongly suggests that government officials and KANU politicians contributed to the organization of the violence, both before and after the violence began, and—ultimately—to impunity for those behind it. Prior to the Likoni attack, raiders testified, men whom they were told were KANU members of parliament (MPs) and key party activists visited their training camps and met with their leaders (and, according to one raider, provided material support). After the raids broke out in Likoni, several top KANU politicians took a number of steps designed to protect the party's interests—even when those interests appeared to conflict with the overriding public interest in ending the raids immediately and bringing those responsible to justice.

Politicians who were not part of government security structures nevertheless closely involved themselves in government security matters by urging a halt to the security operations, according to police testimony, and by pressing for a gun amnesty for raiders. The gun amnesty, as will be discussed, was part of negotiations between the government and the raiders conducted via Shakombo, and provided that the raiders would be pardoned if they handed in the stolen weapons. Politicians also repeatedly interfered in police investigations, undermining accountability for prominent Coast Province politicians who had been implicated in the violence, as well as securing the release of the raiders' spiritual leader (see below). According to testimony from police and judicial authorities, these releases were secured under irregular circumstances and contrary to procedure. In general, security officials said they felt under immense political pressure to comply with the demands of KANU politicians with respect to limiting the security operations and police investigations. Moreover, top politicians associated publicly with the raiders, most notably by asking their spiritual leader to conduct campaign activities on behalf of the ruling party and by providing them material assistance, which they said they did as part of government negotiations to end the raids and recover the stolen guns.

Indications of Early KANU Support

A number of testimonies, most of them from people who claim to have first-hand knowledge of the events, suggest that powerful KANU politicians at the provincial and even national level were deeply involved in the organization of the violence in the Coast region, and some may have been in direct contact with the raiders during the planning phase. The claims are contested or unconfirmed, but taken together raise the possibility that—from the beginning—the Likoni raid and subsequent attacks reflected a violent strategy designed by individuals high up in the ruling party.

In testimony to Human Rights Watch, a former KANU politician in Coast Province described being summoned in 1993 by a senior government official from the Office of the President who expressed concern about KANU's electoral losses in the 1992 election and suggested that the politician mobilize a group to drive out the up-country voters and thereby ensure a KANU win in 1997. (The politician said he did not take up the suggestion.) According to his testimony:

> [The official from the Office of the President] told me that KANU has been threatened by what happened in this [1992] election and that they don't want something like this to happen again because the president might lose. If that trend goes on of up-country people supporting the opposition, it will be dangerous for KANU. He asked me, "How should I take care of them?" He told me that I should form a group like Masumbuko—the official government thug. [...] He said, "Do like Masumbuko and plan something that would make the up-country people leave the area." [...] He meant to do clashes. I know because Masumbuko did that to counter the IPK [Islamic Party of Kenya] by attacking sympathizers [...] I asked him about security and he said, "There's no problem." [...] To make sure if this was official or unofficial, I asked him if the president knows and is aware of it. [The high-level official] said, "We've got the blessings of Mzee [President Moi]." He used those words, in Swahili and English.[219]

A second, consistent account was offered by another former KANU politician, Emmanuel Maitha, who left KANU in late 1997 to run for parliament on the Democratic Party ticket. In December 1997, Maitha gave a newspaper interview in which he was quoted as stating: "The recent 'tribal' clashes at the Coast are part of a larger KANU scheme to rig the December elections."[220] In an interview with the Kenya Human Rights Commission a few days later, he was

---

[219] Human Rights Watch interview with a former KANU politician, Mombasa, May 1999. "Mzee," literally "old man," is sometimes used to refer to the president, as was the case here.
[220] "Clashes: KANU Plot Exposed: Senior Politician Tells of Pre-Poll Rig Scheme," *The Star* (Kenya), December 9-11, 1997, as cited in KHRC, *Killing the Vote: State Sponsored Violence and Flawed Elections in Kenya* (Nairobi: Kenya Human Rights Commission, 1998), pp. 58-9.

more specific, alleging that the Coast violence had been organized by senior KANU politicians. In that interview, Maitha maintained that he was not involved in the raids and claimed that the violence was orchestrated and financed by Rashid Sajjad, an MP and top Coast KANU politician who headed KANU's Coast Province campaign effort, together with a longtime cabinet minister and "associates of theirs at State House [the Office of the President]."[221]

Maitha asserted that the KANU plotters timed the violence to disrupt voting by up-country residents and thereby improve KANU's electoral prospects in the area. According to him, Sajjad took the lead to execute the plan on the ground and the Likoni violence was to be the first stage in a broader KANU strategy to instigate violence for political ends in different parts of Kenya. While Maitha declined to reveal how he learned this, he said he feared for his life because of the sensitive information he had, including first-hand information about prior efforts to disrupt opposition activities (see above).[222] Maitha later maintained that he never spoke to the Kenya Human Rights Commission.[223] Rashid Sajjad categorically rejected the allegations laid to Maitha and asserted the innocence of the other implicated KANU officials.[224] Both Sajjad and the cabinet member implicated in the Maitha interview strongly denied accusations made in parliament and elsewhere that they orchestrated and financed the Likoni raiders' activities.[225]

A statement by Masumbuko was described in police testimony several times at the Akiwumi hearings. For example, the former Coast Province provincial criminal investigations officer, referring both to Masumbuko's statement and one attributed to Maitha (see above), said: "[...T]he statements, in fact, indicated the participation of the two in the previous activities of countering those who were seen

---

[221] KHRC, *Kayas Revisited*, pp. 8-11.

[222] Ibid.

[223] Maitha's testimony to the KHRC was given in the presence of a witness who later described the interview under oath before the Akiwumi Commission. See, for example, Amadi Mugasia and Noel Mwakugu, "Biwott named in clashes probe," *East African Standard*, September 29, 1998. Maitha had argued that he could not have given the interview because he was hospitalized that evening, but hospital records did not corroborate his claim. Akiwumi Commission Official Transcript, October 13, pp. 78-79, 82; Akiwumi Commission Official Transcript, October 14, pp. 122-5; Akiwumi Commission Official Transcript, October 15, p.74.

[224] Kimemia and Sekoh-Ochieng, "How we bought...," *Daily Nation*; Eric Shimoli, "Biwott explains his trip to Coast," *Daily Nation*, August 22, 1997.

[225] "Kenyan opposition blame senior presidential aide for violence," Agence France-Presse, August 21, 1997; "Politics behind Coast chaos," *People*, August 22-28, 1997; Shimoli, "Biwott explains...," *Daily Nation*.

to be having [forming] some other parties like IPK. They also implicated some personalities with whom they were consulting."[226]

Speaking about his experience organizing state-sanctioned violence, while maintaining his innocence with respect to the Likoni violence, Masumbuko's statement reads:

> The issue of burning Likoni Police Station and stealing of guns cannot be done by someone without the assistance of the people in authority. Secondly, this must have taken a long time to plan and also money must have been used. When I used to fight with IPK, the Special Branch [Kenyan police intelligence] was aware of our activity. We used to draw plans together and then I would mobilise the youth to fight. Even this attack on Likoni Police Station must have been the same although it might have gone further to an extent of killing police officers.[227]

Testimony from a raider provides a different perspective, but one that also supports the charge that the raiders received support from important KANU leaders and allies as they were preparing for their planned attacks. According to an early recruit, politicians visited the camps and invoked the name of "Mzee" (President Moi) to suggest, rightly or wrongly, political support at the highest level.[228]

He stated further that he did not know these visitors, but that his commanders identified them as KANU members of parliament (MPs) and key party activists from Coast Province. Some of the visitors, he added, provided direct support to the raiders in advance of the raids. He said that one person was a particularly frequent political visitor, whom he personally witnessed at the camp four times before the Likoni raid. This person met with the raiders' local leaders and also exchanged greetings with the outsiders. After the visitor left, the raiders would receive food

---

[226] Akiwumi Commission Official Transcript, June 9, 1999, pp. 54-55. See also, for example, Akiwumi Commission Official Transcript, October 14, 1998, pp. 76-78.

[227] "Likoni clashes: A personal account," *People*, November 7, 2001, read together with "Last of the people who should be investigated," *People*, November 16, 2001; Akiwumi Commission Official Transcript, October 14, 1998, pp. 76-78; Akiwumi Commission Official Transcript, June 9, 1999, pp. 54-55.

[228] Human Rights Watch interview with Raider A, Ukunda, April 22, 1999. One raider interviewed by KHRC stated that he was told he would be trained to be part of the security arrangement for "Mzee" during the 1997 general elections, clarifying that in that case also, the term refers to the president. KHRC, *Kayas of Deprivation*, p. 23.

delivered by pickup truck. The raider also stated that the visitor provided the raiders with a lorry the night of the Likoni raid to transport them to the site of the attack. The raider also explained that after several of these visits, the leaders would indicate that they had been given money or even a few guns (which he said were wrapped in a package so they were not visible). He added that all of the visits, even when not accompanied by direct support, served to encourage the raiders because they demonstrated that the raiders had the backing of important people.[229]

In addition, Swaleh bin Alfan testified before the Akiwumi Commission that Shakombo and Sajjad visited his home together a few days prior to the Likoni raid. He said the two men told him they had some people in the forest who were organizing for violence and that he should keep this information secret. During the visit, Alfan added, three other visitors arrived and were introduced as leaders of the raiders, including Bempa. Alfan further stated that he witnessed Shakombo and Sajjad give money to these three men, Ksh.3,000 (U.S.$50), to buy food. Alfan retracted these statements in subsequent testimony before the Akiwumi Commission. When speaking to Human Rights Watch in 1999 he maintained that his initial testimony, which both Sajjad and Shakombo strongly rejected, had been correct.[230]

A number of allegations surfaced that Shakombo was intimately involved in the raiders' planning activities. For example, a KANU politician, Suleiman Kamole, testified to the Akiwumi Commission that he attended a security meeting after the Likoni raid in which Alfan declared that Shakombo had been the one who took prospective raiders to him to be oathed.[231] Shakombo was also named as a

---

[229] Human Rights Watch interview with Raider A, Mombasa, May 21, 1999. Raiders interviewed by KHRC similarly reported that they saw visitors at the training camp and, while they did not know them, they were identified as KANU politicians. KHRC, *Kayas of Deprivation*, pp. 22, 24.

[230] Human Rights Watch interview with Swaleh bin Alfan, Denyenye, May 25, 1999; Akiwumi Commission Official Transcript, August 31, 1998, pp. 81, 89-92; Akiwumi Commission Official Transcript, October 16, 1998, pp. 24-26; Akiwumi Commission Official Transcript, October 28, 1998, pp. 34, 37. For other accounts of Alfan's testimony, see, for example, Patrick Mayoyo and Michael Mumo, "PC, Sajjad 'held meetings with Likoni raid suspect," *Daily Nation*, September 1, 1998; Michael Mumo and Patrick Mayoyo, "Oathing suspect contradicts himself," *Daily Nation*, September 2, 1998. Sajjad's lawyer objected to the taking of Alfan's testimony on this point. Akiwumi Commission Official Transcript, August 31, 1998, p. 88.

[231] "Saga of beach plots," *Daily Nation*, November 7, 1998. Kamole added that at the meeting Shakombo strongly denied the statement, but Alfan insisted it was true. Shakombo, as noted below, denied any involvement in the raiders' activities.

supplier of weapons to the raiders in advance of the Likoni attack.[232] Moreover, Shakombo was alleged before the Akiwumi Commission to have financed the raiders during the planning phase, based on information provided to police by a captured raider who stated that the politician gave raiders Ksh.27,000 [$490] in two payments in February 1997.[233] In addition, police said several suspects told them that Shakombo incited them to attack the Likoni police station and expel up-country residents from the area.[234] Shakombo, who testified that he had family ties to the raiders, acknowledged that he was aware of the raiders' oathing and training activities, as well as their plans to attack police stations in order to acquire weapons, which he reported to a local intelligence officer in May 1997, but by his account he had absolutely no part in them.[235]

KANU Politicians Seek Halt to Security Operations

In mid-August, 1997, only a few days after the Likoni police station attack, members of the provincial security committee (PSC) held a meeting, jointly with other officials, to discuss ongoing security operations. Three officials who participated told the Akiwumi Commission that Sajjad and Maitha appeared at the office of the provincial police officer (PPO) as their meeting was in progress. They said the politicians made clear that they wanted operations against the raiders to cease and cited political reasons. Maitha agreed only that he had told the PSC members that abuses by government forces against the Digo and the wider Mijikenda population risked undermining support for KANU in the election later that year. His testimony to the commission differed slightly in other respects. He stated that his objection to the security operation was the involvement of the military and the manner in which police were conducting searches, but said he did not call for an end to all operations. He also said that he was speaking only for himself, on behalf of the Mijikenda community. The security officials further

---

[232] KHRC, *Kayas of Deprivation*, p. 24; KHRC, *Kayas Revisited*, p. 17.

[233] Akiwumi Commission Official Transcript, October 6, 1998, pp. 13, 23-24. See also, Mugasia, "Raid thought...," *East African Standard*; Michael Mumo and Patrick Mayoyo, "Police boss 'ordered Mwidau's release," *Daily Nation*, October 7, 1998.

[234] Akiwumi Commission Official Transcript, October 15, 1998, p. 126. The senior official on the stand read from a police report identifying Shakombo as a suspect. See below.

[235] Akiwumi Commission Official Transcript, October 28, 1998, especially pp. 2-3, 6, 18, 113-115. See also, for example, Boniface Kaona and Michael Githua, "Shakombo says he visited Likoni raiders in the forests," *East African Standard*, October 29, 1998; Watoro Kamau, "MP denies funding youth training camp," *Daily Nation*, October 30, 1998. Shakombo's contacts with the raiders following the August 13, 1997, Likoni attack is described below.

stated that Sajjad implicitly endorsed the call to end the operations, which Sajjad denied through his lawyer. Regardless, Sajjad's presence at the meeting likely made a difference, as at the time he was considered a very powerful figure in Coast Province. Perceptions of his level of influence were such that Sajjad was twice alleged before the Akiwumi Commission to have directed government affairs in Coast Province (a claim rejected by the officials on the stand).[236]

This was not the only such incident on which security officials testified. For example, one senior official said that KANU MPs Boy and Mwamzandi also pressed for an end to the security operation, again citing abuses against their constituents. Both denied that they wanted the operations halted and said that they instead complained about how the operations were conducted.[237]

Shakombo, at that time still with KANU, testified that he met with President Moi in Mombasa approximately one week after the outbreak of violence in Coast Province to protest the conduct of security officials. He said he recommended at that meeting that the government offer a pardon to encourage raiders to hand in the stolen weapons. The government soon thereafter announced a gun amnesty, with President Moi announcing a week-long amnesty on August 22 and later extending it by ten days until September 9. In December 1997, with only twenty-four of the stolen guns recovered, President Moi said he would consider granting amnesty to the more than 200 suspects charged in connection with the violence if the remainder of the guns were handed in. The balance of the weapons were not surrendered and the amnesty was not granted.[238]

The effect of the August-September amnesty was to contribute to further chaos and displacement. Police officials indicated that the amnesty effectively suspended security operations against the raiders—who were operating from camps in the Kaya Bombo forest and Similani caves—for nearly one month.[239] But many

---

[236] Akiwumi Commission Official Transcript, October 6, 1998, pp. 59-62, 68; Akiwumi Commission Official Transcript, October 12, 1998, pp. 85-91; Akiwumi Commission Official Transcript, October 13, pp. 68-72; Akiwumi Commission Official Transcript, October 15, 1998, pp. 32-52; Pekeshe and Mugasia, "Kisauni MP denies...," *East African Standard*; Amadi Mugasia, "Nassir sought release of key clashes suspect, says ex-cop," *East African Standard*, October 15, 1998.

[237] Akiwumi Commission Official Transcript, October 14, 1998, pp. 45-46, 155-156; Akiwumi Commission Official Transcript, October 23, 1998, pp. 56, 69; Mugasia, "Nassir sought...," *East African Standard*.

[238] Watoro Kamau, "MP 'met' Moi over police harassment," *Daily Nation*, October 29, 1998; "Moi: 24 guns still missing," *Daily Nation*, December 23, 1997.

[239] Mayoyo and Mumo, "Ex-police boss...," *Daily Nation*; Ngumbao Kithi and Michael Mumo, "Witness links man to oathing," *Daily Nation*, September 23, 1998.

residents of the Coast region continued to fear security forces who, during the amnesty period in particular, conducted sweeps in residential areas and targeted Digo residents for unlawful arrest and mistreatment, and therefore joined up-country residents in fleeing their homes. As one raider put it, "KANU gave people ten days to return the guns or threaten an ambush, so the civilians had to leave."[240]

Political Interference in Police Investigations

Amid accusations from many quarters that the bloodshed was politically motivated, intended to influence the election results and disrupt the political momentum of the constitutional reform movement, government and ruling party officials repeatedly sought to deflect attention from allegations concerning KANU politicians by pointing the finger at their political rivals. The August 15 arrest of a human rights investigator, an opposition party activist, and a politician from a Coast-based unregistered party, on charges of unlawful assembly, fit into this strategy.[241]

KANU politicians, for their part, accused the opposition of sparking the violence to damage KANU's reputation. The leader of KANU explained the party's position: "The clashes must have been started by somebody who knew they would make KANU unpopular and who believed they could get away with simply blaming them on KANU. Nobody should go for votes by killing people and then blaming his political opponent. That is immoral."[242] President Moi stated: "KANU is a party which advocates peace and unity and at no time can it perpetrate violence."[243] He and the KANU leader both strongly condemned the violence and firmly asserted that any politician found to have been involved would be arrested,

---

[240] Human Rights Watch interview with Raider B, Mombasa, May 26, 1999.

[241] Two of those charged (Alamin Mazrui of KHRC and Khelef Khalifa, then a Safina Party activist) were released from custody. The third person, Ali Chizondo of the unregistered Coast-based National Democratic Union (NADU) party, was charged in connection with the violence and denied bail (see below).

[242] Margaretta wa Gacheru, "Sunkuli: We're all concerned about the damage," *Daily Nation*, September 28, 1997.

[243] "Churchmen blame Govt over mayhem," *Daily Nation*, August 24, 1997.

with Moi stating: "Even if you are an MP you won't escape if you incite people."[244] In practice, however, political considerations very much inhibited police investigations, and ultimately these promises were at best empty words.

Police officials testified that they became suspicious about the role of KANU members in the violence. In some cases, they said suspects implicated KANU politicians as organizers of the violence. In other cases, police suspected ruling party politicians because they sought to interfere in the police investigation, including by calling for an end to the security operation. They also indicated that they developed doubts about politicians who gained access to the raiders to help arrange the return of guns. In still other cases politicians were named as police suspects on the basis of allegations linking them to the raiders. Among those named as suspects by police for one or more of these reasons were Boy, Maitha, Masumbuko, Mwahima, Mwamzandi, Hisham Mwidau (see list, above), and Shakombo.[245] The provincial criminal investigations officer at the time of the Likoni raid, during cross-examination by a lawyer representing the Law Society of Kenya, agreed with the lawyer that there was no reason why Shakombo had not been arrested and charged.[246] He also agreed that there should have been an investigation of higher-ranking KANU members who were implicated, including Sajjad, in particular to gather statements from them concerning the allegations.[247] This, however, was not done.

Francis Gichuki, who headed up the Coast Province police team as the PPO at the time, commented at the Akiwumi hearings that in some cases arrests were not

---

[244] Ibid; "Politics behind coast chaos," *People*, August 22-28, 1997. In a press interview published on the day before the 1997 election, Moi allowed that KANU may have been involved, saying: "It is my belief that politicians on both sides (of the political divide) instigated the violence as a means of making political capital and embarrassing my Government, especially with regard to tourism." Bernard Nderitu, "Interview with President Moi," *Daily Nation*, Africa News Service, December 28, 1997.

[245] Akiwumi Commission Official Transcript, October 6, 1998, pp. 65, 69-70, 90; Akiwumi Commission Official Transcript, October 7, 1998, pp. 4, 42-43, 78; Akiwumi Commission Official Transcript, October 8, 1998, p. 22; Akiwumi Commission Official Transcript, October 14, 1998, pp. 76-77, 134-36; Mumo and Mayoyo, "Move to derail...," *Daily Nation*; Mugasia, "Police differed...," *East African Standard*; Mugasia, "Raid thought...," *East African Standard*; Michael Mumo, "Clashes Inquiry faces a cash hitch," *Daily Nation*, October 8, 1998; Pekeshe and Mugasia, "Kisauni MP denies...," *East African Standard*; "Six more killed, leaflets target groups," *Daily Nation*, African News Service, August 18, 1997.

[246] Akiwumi Commission Official Transcript, October 12, 1998, p. 50.

[247] Akiwumi Commission Official Transcript, October 12, 1998, p. 50.

made because the suspects were politically well-connected and some served in the government. As he put it, "I did not want to burn my fingers."[248]

In the case of Masumbuko, Gichuki testified that police suspected Masumbuko because he was the first to arrive at the scene of raids, as if he knew in advance where they would take place. Other sources have alleged that Masumbuko was responsible for recruiting the highly trained outsiders who helped the raiders. He was suspected in part because of his role in organizing and training local youths under UMA (as noted, one raider said former UMA members joined their ranks). In a rare instance of police action against a politically connected suspect, the KANU activist was arrested on August 20, 1997, charged in connection with the violence, and prosecuted.[249]

As police themselves testified, a high level of political interference in judicial matters concerning the Coast violence undermined accountability, and prominent suspects were unlikely to face arrest, much less prosecution. Indeed, several politicians who were arrested in connection with the violence were released from custody after top officials intervened on their behalf, and in some of those cases KANU political interests were explicitly cited as a reason for their release. The circumstances and conditions of these releases were not always made clear, but in most cases the evidence suggests the politicians were released without charge or that charges were later dropped.

In a notable example, a police officer reportedly motivated by political considerations arranged for Maitha to be released on bond two weeks after his arrest. The provincial criminal investigations officer (PCIO) acknowledged that he instructed prosecuting and judicial officers to charge Maitha with a bailable offense, as opposed to a more serious charge he might otherwise have faced. According to the magistrate and the police prosecutor, the PCIO told them that top officials had determined that this move was necessary to protect the interests of the ruling party. Both recalled that the PCIO explained that the continued detention of Maitha, who was still with KANU at the time, could cause the party to lose votes among Mijikenda supporters. They also both said that the PCIO told them that the decision to release Maitha on bond had been reached at a provincial security meeting with the president, but the PCIO strongly denied that he had invoked President Moi's name or attributed the decision to the provincial security committee; instead, he testified that he was acting on an order from the Kenyan commissioner of police in Nairobi. The police commissioner denied that that was

---

[248] Akiwumi Commission Official Transcript, October 14, 1998, p. 47.

[249] Akiwumi Commission Official Transcript, October 14, 1998, p. 77; "Six more killed...," *Daily Nation.*

the case, and PSC members also disassociated themselves completely from the PCIO's action.[250]

Political interference also influenced the case of Mwalimu Masoud Mwahima, who was a KANU councillor and later would become Mombasa's mayor, as well as that of Hisham Mwidau, the KANU MP candidate for Likoni. Both men were arrested on suspicion of involvement in the Likoni violence. In the case of Mwidau, police arrested him on evidence that his vehicle had been used to transport raiders. Mwahima, according to police testimony, was similarly suspected of allowing his vehicle to be used by raiders and, moreover, was the subject of unconfirmed allegations that raiders fired shots from a house belonging to him. The investigating officer from Nairobi, who had ordered the arrests, testified that the PCIO arranged to release both suspects without his consent. According to testimony at the Akiwumi hearings, the politicians were released without charge. Political pressure had been brought to bear in this case; the former PPO testified that Mwidau's release was the result of "negotiations," and that cabinet minister and Coast Province MP Shariff Nassir pressed for Mwahima to be

---

[250] Akiwumi Commission Official Transcript, October 2, 1998, pp. 20-22, 28-33; Akiwumi Commission Official Transcript, October 6, 1998, pp. 74-76, 78-82; Akiwumi Commission Official Transcript, October 12, 1998, p. 99-102; Akiwumi Commission Official Transcript, June 4, 1999, pp. 1-2; Pekeshe and Mugasia, "Kisauni MP denies...," *East African Standard*; Mumo, "Clashes Inquiry...," *Daily Nation*; Michael Mumo and Ngumbao Kithi, "Likoni: PC in a spot," *Daily Nation*, October 9, 1998; Amadi Mugasia, "Officer wanted Maitha freed, says magistrate," *East African Standard*, October 3, 1998; Michael Mumo and Patrick Mayoyo, "President 'ordered Maitha release,'" *Daily Nation*, October 3, 1999. Maitha, who maintained that he was innocent of the charges filed, denied any involvement with the raiders. Akiwumi Commission Official Transcript, October 12, 1998, p. 115.

released from custody. The minister confirmed this in his testimony before the Akiwumi Commission.[251]

One case of political interference stands out because police strongly believed the prisoner, Swaleh bin Alfan, was a prime suspect; yet he was released from custody after he had been charged with non-bailable offenses. Several top security officials testified that from the time of Alfan's arrest on August 15, they were under great pressure from various politicians—including former assistant minister Mwamzandi, former KANU MP Boy, and then-KANU aspirant to a parliamentary seat Shakombo—to release him from custody, ostensibly so he could use his influence to promote the surrender of weapons stolen by the raiders.[252]

Shakombo openly acknowledged playing a key role in arranging Alfan's release. Shakombo testified that, acting through a cousin who was associated with the raiders, he urged the raiders to hand in the stolen weapons under the gun amnesty, and they in turn demanded that Alfan be released. He said he personally visited the raiders' hideout in the Similani caves to deliver the message that the authorities had agreed to the raiders' conditions. There was a delay, however, and Alfan was first taken to remand prison at Shimo la Tewa, north of Mombasa. This seeming betrayal of the promise made to the raiders put the strategy at risk, he

---

[251] Akiwumi Commission Official Transcript, October 6, 1998, pp. 32-43; Akiwumi Commission Official Transcript, October 7, 1998, pp. 43-44; Akiwumi Commission Official Transcript, October 14, 1998, pp. 41-45, 54, 119-120, 135-137; Akiwumi Commission Official Transcript, October 15, 1998, pp. 15-16; Akiwumi Commission Official Transcript, October 23, 1998, pp. 91-96; Akiwumi Commission Official Transcript, June 4, 1999, pp. 1-2; Francis Thoya, "Sajjad named in Likoni case," *Daily Nation*, June 30, 1998; Michael Mumo and Patrick Mayoyo, "MPs to appear at clashes Inquiry," *Daily Nation*, October 15, 1998; Mugasia, "Nassir sought...," *East African Standard*; "Witness blames ex-PPO for escalation of Likoni clashes," *East African Standard*, September 10, 1998; Mumo and Kithi, "Likoni: Officer says...," *Daily Nation*; Patrick Mayoyo and Michael Mumo, "Ex-MP 'collected names of youths,'" *Daily Nation*, September 11, 1998. As noted above, Mwahima denied having any connection to the raiders. Mwidau also maintained his innocence, maintaining (as did his driver) that his vehicle was hijacked. KHRC, *Kayas Revisited*, pp. 16-18.

[252] See, for example, Akiwumi Commission Official Transcript, October 6, 1998, p. 55; Akiwumi Commission Official Transcript, October 14, 1998, p. 157-60; Mugasia, "Nassir sought...," *East African Standard*; Jacinta Sekoh-Ochieng and Maguta Kimemia, "Clashes judge Ondeyo accuses Nassir," *Daily Nation*, October 24, 1998.

added, and resulted in the killing of his cousin by the angry raiders. Out of concern for his own safety, he said, he cut off contact with the raiders.[253]

Alfan's release, however, would soon be secured. During a visit to the province in the third week of August, President Moi announced that the government would arrange for the oath administrator (not named) to withdraw the oath under official supervision. The following month a PSC meeting was held on September 22 with Coast political leaders. Those present, which included a number of prominent KANU MPs, aspiring MPs, and civic leaders—some of whom had themselves been implicated in the violence—pressed for Alfan's release, arguing that he be set free to de-oath the raiders. According to officials, the provincial security team had earlier rejected the same appeal from various politicians, but under continued pressure the PSC reversed its initial decision. One factor was that some of the PSC members who had voted against the measure before had by then been transferred and replaced. When asked why Alfan, charged with the crime of oathing, was set free to carry out an act, de-oathing, that is also illegal under Kenyan law, one of the new PSC members stated that it this was the "unanimous agreement" of the PSC and the political leaders.[254]

Three days later, on September 25, Alfan was ordered released on bail on the recommendation of the prosecution. The then-director of the Criminal Investigations Department in Nairobi testified that he was consulted in advance and did not object to the PSC's decision. To make his release possible, the new Coast Province PCIO (in place since the mid-September transfer of his predecessor) instructed that capital charges against Alfan be dropped. Alfan's bond of

---

[253] Statement Under Inquiry dated February 28, 1998, copy on file with Human Rights Watch; Akiwumi Commission Official Transcript, October 12, 1998, pp. 35-37; Kaona and Githua, "Shakombo says...," *East African Standard.* Shakombo testified that Bempa, the raiders' leader, was also his cousin.

[254] Akiwumi Commission Official Transcript, October 16, 1998, pp. 58-64; Akiwumi Commission Official Transcript, October 6, 1998, p. 55; Akiwumi Commission Official Transcript, October 14, 1998, p. 157-60; Mugasia, "Nassir sought...," *East African Standard*; Sekoh-Ochieng and Kimemia, "Clashes judge...," *Daily Nation.*

Ksh.200,000 ($3,360) was put up by no less a figure than MP Boy, who confirmed this, and Alfan claimed Sajjad and Shakombo had arranged this assistance.[255] Senior police officials appeared eager to keep Alfan out of jail. When Alfan was arrested on fresh evidence in November, the new PPO ordered Alfan be freed immediately, saying he wanted Alfan out of jail so the police could monitor his activities. The arresting officer, however, said he worried that the arrest had antagonized powerful individuals and requested a transfer because he feared for his life as a result.[256]

KANU Campaigns with the Raiders' Spiritual Leader

After politicians arranged for Alfan's release and until he was rearrested and jailed on similar charges following the December 1997 elections, Alfan was recruited to help KANU politicians campaign and was given money for this purpose. His help was enlisted by Suleiman Kamole and the provincial commissioner (PC). The latter said an official in the Office of the President instructed him to work with Alfan to arrange de-oathing of the raiders.[257]

Notably, no such de-oathing ever took place after Alfan's release. Alfan testified that he did not carry out any such ceremony, and security officials said they believed that, to the contrary, Alfan administered more oaths once he was

---

[255] Akiwumi Commission Official Transcript, October 16, 1998, pp. 67-68; Akiwumi Commission Official Transcript, August 31, 1998, pp. 70-81; Akiwumi Commission Official Transcript, May 31, 1999, pp. 110-113; Sekoh-Ochieng and Kimemia, "Clashes judge...," Daily Nation; Patrick Mayoyo and Michael Mumo, "Oathing suspect links MPs to clashes," Daily Nation, October 17, 1998. Sajjad strongly rejected Alfan's claim that he and Shakombo visited the spiritual leader in police custody and promised to have him released, while Shakombo acknowledged visiting Alfan in jail together with government officials, but said Sajjad was not with them. Akiwumi Commission Official Transcript, October 28, 1998, pp. 33, 62; Ochieng, "Likoni: Sajjad...," Daily Nation; Kaona and Githua, "Shakombo says...," East African Standard.

[256] Mayoyo and Nyaga, "Ex-MPs attended...," Daily Nation; "I was scared after release of a suspect, DO tells team," East African Standard, September 26, 1998.

[257] Akiwumi Commission Official Transcript, November 5, 1998, pp. 142-146; Boniface Kaona and Michael Githua, "Biwott, Saitoti to face inquiry," East African Standard, November 4, 1998; Watoro Kamau and Mark Agutu, "Judge: Ex-PC abused office," Daily Nation, November 4, 1998.

released.[258] According to Shakombo, Alfan told him that he would not stop oathing the raiders until majimbo was introduced.[259] The then-PPO stated that when Alfan was rearrested and charged in early 1998, following the elections, it was because they had discovered that he was not carrying out de-oathing ceremonies, as agreed.[260] Both Shakombo and Boy, however, testified that this was known already in November, when Alfan was briefly arrested and immediately released (on the orders of the same PPO), and said that they had by then personally conveyed news of fresh oathing by Alfan to security officials.[261]

It was established at the Akiwumi Commission that Sajjad and Kamole gave Alfan a large sum of money, Ksh.700,000 ($11,800), in two installments paid in Sajjad's office, as well as use of a vehicle, to campaign for KANU.[262] Kamole, asked at the Akiwumi hearings if it was not wrong to have "used a murder to achieve your cause," replied: "If this was looked [seen] in a negative way it is bad. For us we did our best to ensure KANU won the election."[263] He and Sajjad (who, strikingly, claimed he was unaware of accusations against Alfan at the time) both felt that Alfan's influence in Kwale could help KANU win votes and said their intention in giving him funds was that they should be used to "buy votes" and for

---

[258] Human Rights Watch interview with Swaleh bin Alfan, Denyenye, May 25, 1999; Akiwumi Commission Official Transcript, May 31, 1999, p. 113; Akiwumi Commission Official Transcript, October 15, 1998, pp. 27, 104-5; Akiwumi Commission Official Transcript, October 16, 1998, pp. 78-82.

[259] Akiwumi Commission Official Transcript, October 28, 1998, pp. 38-39; Kaona and Githua, "Shakombo says...," *East African Standard.*

[260] Akiwumi Commission Official Transcript, October 16, 1998, p. 78-82.

[261] Akiwumi Commission Official Transcript, October 29, 1998, p. 63-65; Akiwumi Commission Official Transcript, October 23, 1998, pp. 74, 83; Sekoh-Ochieng and Kimemia, "Clashes judge...," *Daily Nation.*

[262] Akiwumi Commission Official Transcript, August 31, 1998, pp. 83-85; "Saga of beach...," *Daily Nation*; Kimemia and Sekoh-Ochieng, "How we bought...," *Daily Nation.* See also Akiwumi Commission Official Transcript, November 5, 1998, pp. 134-146. Kamole also testified that during the period before KANU nominations, when Sajjad was not yet able to release campaign funds, Kamole had independently arranged to give Alfan some money to secure his later assistance with the campaign, referring to payments of "Ksh.5,000 here and Ksh.7,000 there." Akiwumi Commission Official Transcript, November 5, 1998, pp. 53, 142-143. The sums listed were equivalent to approximately $82 and $115 at the time, respectively.

[263] "Saga of beach...," *Daily Nation.*

other campaign expenses.[264] For his part, Alfan agreed that the money was ostensibly meant to have been used for campaign activities, but testified that he passed the first payment of Ksh.400,000 ($6,730) to the raiders for them to spend directly.[265] (The raiders themselves were aware that politicians funneled them money via Alfan, as described below.)

Alfan said that, in exchange for promises of additional money, he spoke at numerous KANU rallies and mobilized the Digo vote for the ruling party in the general election. He testified that he campaigned for KANU candidates even though he believed the politicians were linked to the violence under Sajjad's leadership.[266] Alfan also testified that Sajjad promised him monetary rewards for his electoral help.[267]

Politicians Assist the Raiders During the Ongoing Clashes

Beyond what raiders described about visits from politicians as they prepared for violence, Human Rights Watch obtained important new information about the involvement of politicians after the violence was unleashed. In first-hand testimonies, raiders told Human Rights Watch that prominent politicians visited them during this period. According to the raiders, these politicians provided food and money during ongoing clashes. Based on these visits, the aid these politicians provided, and statements by the raiders' leaders to the effect that they had powerful political backers, some of the raiders believed they benefited from political sponsorship for their continued activities—and ultimately, rewards for phasing them out. After raids in August 1997 led to the large-scale displacement of the up-country population in affected areas, politicians encouraged the raiders to halt the raids in exchange for jobs or assistance to leave the country. In some cases the raiders interpreted this offer of continued assistance as a reward for their work so far and a sign that the violence had gone on too long and had become a liability, not as an indicator that the politicians objected to their actions. To the contrary,

---

[264] Kimemia and Sekoh-Ochieng, "How we bought...," *Daily Nation*; "Saga of beach...," *Daily Nation*. See also Akiwumi Commission Official Transcript, November 5, 1998, pp. 134-142.

[265] Akiwumi Commission Official Transcript, August 31, 1998, pp. 86-87; Mayoyo and Mumo, "Oathing suspect links...," *Daily Nation*; Human Rights Watch interview with Swaleh bin Alfan, Denyenye, May 25, 1999.

[266] Mayoyo and Mumo, "Oathing suspect links...," *Daily Nation*.

[267] Akiwumi Commission Official Transcript, August 31, 1998, pp. 85-86. He repeated this assertion in a later interview with Human Rights Watch. Human Rights Watch interview with Swaleh bin Alfan, Denyenye, May 25, 1999.

raiders attributed comments to politicians endorsing the goal of majimbo even in the midst of the violence. Allegations also surfaced during the Akiwumi Commission hearings that prominent politicians provided material and financial support, as well as political backing, to the raiders in their hideouts even during the period of active violence. As noted, the implicated politicians, for their part, have publicly denied they supported the raiders' agenda and offered their own accounts of their interactions with them.

During the ongoing clashes, the raiders said, they received direct gifts of food from several politicians, as well as money, most of which they used to buy food. In some cases, the raiders claim that politicians personally delivered such support to the raiders at the hideouts. One raider who helped guard the raiders' camp in the Similani caves stated that he saw Boy and Shakombo visit the hideout together twice. On a third occasion, he stated, Shakombo arrived with another man he did not recognize. The raider was not able to see clearly whether money changed hands during these meetings, but after the visitors left the camp, each time his commanders would announce that they had received money for food.[268]

Another raider, interviewed separately, also stated that he repeatedly saw Boy and Shakombo at the raiders' hideout and added that they brought food for the raiders. He did not indicate that he saw them give money, but he testified that during their visits, "they would say, 'When we get majimbo you will get money from the boss,'" leading to the conclusion that they supported the raiders' cause and backed their actions.[269]

The raiders also described receiving food deliveries arranged by politicians, especially Shakombo. For example, one raider stated that Shakombo arranged for his cousin, who had facilitated the surrender of some weapons, to deliver food to the hideouts.[270] Often, the raiders added, their food supplies were paid for with money Swaleh bin Alfan said had been furnished by politicians.[271] For example, a raider stated: "We would get our food by sending boys [youths] to Swaleh's house." He also stated that Swaleh told him, "Tomorrow I will go and get money from Shakombo and Juma Boy."[272]

Alfan was among those who, speaking before the Akiwumi Commission, similarly alleged that politicians aided the raiders in the period after the attack on

---

[268] Human Rights Watch interview with Raider D, Mombasa, May 9, 1999.

[269] Human Rights Watch interview with Raider C, Mombasa, May 9, 1999.

[270] Human Rights Watch interview with Raider B, Mombasa, May 26, 1999.

[271] Human Rights Watch interviews with Raider B and Raider C, Coast Province, May 1999.

[272] Human Rights Watch interview with Raider D, Mombasa, May 9, 1999.

the Likoni police station. He testified, for example, that Shakombo sent food to the raiders, and alleged that Boy was among the politicians who provided financial support to the raiders after August 13, 1997.[273] As noted above, police testified that several suspects named Shakombo as a financier and vocal supporter of their cause from an early stage.

Both Shakombo and Boy denied the accusations. In his account, Boy said that he was in contact with raiders only indirectly, through two campaign managers. He stated that security officials approached him asking for help contacting the raiders to arrange the surrender of the guns stolen by the raiders. Boy denied that he had known of the raiders' activities before the Likoni attack or that he at any point financed the raiders or visited them. He also rejected claims that he supported the raiders' political agenda, the ousting of up-country residents and institution of a majimbo system of governance.[274]

Shakombo, for his part, confirmed to the Akiwumi Commission that he had direct and close contact with the raiders, but testified that he was working on behalf of security officials—to arrange the surrender of guns. In that capacity, he said, he visited the raiders in their hideout on one occasion, spoke to their commander (Bempa, his cousin) and greeted the raiders, whom he estimated numbered as many as 300. In a published interview he gave to the Kenya Human Rights Commission in December 1997, Shakombo added further detail. In that interview he said that, acting as negotiator on behalf of the government, he was granted police permission to provide the raiders with food and medicine and that he had arranged to purchase supplies and have them delivered to the raiders in his car. He stated further that the police gave him some funds for this purpose, doled out in relatively small amounts of Ksh.5,000-10,000 ($85-$170). Shakombo later denied having given the KHRC interview even after being told by the Akiwumi Commission that KHRC had audio-recorded it and that, in any case, his testimony at the hearings was highly consistent with what he told the KHRC.[275]

---

[273] Akiwumi Commission Official Transcript, October 15, 1998, p. 117; Akiwumi Commission Official Transcript, October 16, 1998, pp. 10, 12.

[274] Akiwumi Commission Official Transcript, October 23, 1998, pp. 17-20, 48-51, 71, 126.

[275] Akiwumi Commission Official Transcript, October 28, 1998, especially pp. 16-18, 28-32, 56, 108-124; KHRC, *Kayas Revisited*, pp. 18-30; Kaona and Githua, "Shakombo says...," *East African Standard*. Speaking in another context, Shakombo also strongly denied financing the raiders' activities. Kamau, "MP denies funding...," *Daily Nation*. Regarding the KHRC interview, Shakombo denied that he would have implicated Sajjad, as was published by KHRC, but allowed that an interview could have been recorded without his knowledge. Akiwumi Commission Official Transcript, October 29, 1998, pp. 13-14.

Some of the raiders felt that, especially as the attacks wore on, politicians provided support in order to coopt the raiders and encourage them to halt their attacks, sometimes linking the desire to see the violence end to the upcoming elections. For example, a raider told Human Rights Watch that he met with Boy at Alfan's house, and, according to his testimony, "He said to cool down so the elections could take place." He added, "Shakombo's group was at first the same as Boy's," meaning that at the time "Shakombo was [with] KANU."[276] According to this raider, "Shakombo came to the bush and said, 'What you've done is enough.'"[277] However, the same raider stated that the raiders refused to be coopted and used the money indirectly supplied by politicians for their own purposes. He said, "Some of the senior people came to cool us down after the operation [the Likoni attack], to give us food," but "we used it for other reasons [purposes]."[278] The raider also said he did not take seriously the government's offer of a gun amnesty and believed it was another ploy by politicians to coopt the raiders for their own purposes. He said Shakombo and others offered the raiders incentives such as jobs to cooperate, and that a former provincial official promised them that they would be designated "homeguards" (referring to members of the Kenya Police Reserve program) and given new guns if they handed in their weapons.

The Electoral Pay-off for KANU

From the perspective of the election results, the incitement of violence against up-country residents, the majority of whom were known to support the opposition, was a complete success. The KHRC, which carried out an analysis of the December 29, 1997, election results, showed that the areas where up-country people were targeted for attack corresponded to the areas where the concentration of registered up-country voters was highest. By KHRC estimates, at least 75 percent of up-country voters in these areas were displaced by the violence and many of them lost needed identity documents, making it impossible for them to vote even if they returned to the Coast Province constituency where they were registered. Of the displaced people who had returned to the Coast region, they found many remained too scared to vote, in part because of continued threats from indigenous residents.[279]

There were seven parliamentary seats up for election in the two districts most affected by the Coast violence, four in Mombasa district and three in Kwale

---

[276] Human Rights Watch interview with Raider B, Mombasa, May 26, 1999.
[277] Ibid.
[278] Human Rights Watch interview with Raider B, Ukunda, May 8, 1999.
[279] KHRC, *Killing the Vote*, pp. 67-73.

district. With the 1997 vote, KANU picked up one additional seat in Mombasa and retained two others, while retaining all three seats in Kwale. In the presidential vote, President Moi swept the province. The president's electoral support improved markedly as compared to 1992, KHRC found, even in areas considered opposition strongholds. In Likoni, Moi brought in 41.5 percent of the vote, more than a ten-point rise from his 1992 tally. In Mombasa district as a whole, votes for Moi rose eight percentage points over 1992 levels.[280]

KANU leaders said the results validated their claim that KANU was not responsible for the violence and, in doing so, ignored the effect on the vote of the displacement of up-country voters. One typical statement emphasized the ruling party's concern that widespread police abuses in residential areas might have caused the party to lose support among the Digo community, but noted that KANU performed very well regardless. In it, then-KANU councillor Mwahima, who had been implicated in the violence, as noted, stated:

> KANU did not harm anybody. But, it was the opposition; the
> security people who were brought here wanted to sully the image
> of KANU. And we were very worried because...that...we would
> lose the seats in the area. But, fortunately, the people
> understood. There were four civic seats [in the Likoni
> constituency], we got three, and lost one. We lost the
> parliamentary seat, and that was out of sheer bad luck. We did
> not lose it because KANU had been rejected...And the president
> won many votes in our area demonstrating once again that the
> people were aware that KANU was not responsible for what
> happened.[281]

The Likoni parliamentary seat went to Shakombo, who was defeated for the KANU nomination and won under the Shirikisho Party of Kenya, a Coast-based pro-*majimbo* party. The party was initially denied registration, but in the wake of the Likoni violence and amid concerns that KANU might lose the vote in Likoni district in the upcoming election, it was allowed to register on November 18,

---

[280] Ibid, pp. 73, 83.

[281] KHRC, *Kayas Revisited*, p. 14. In denying allegations that KANU had instigated the violence, Sajjad stated that he and other party figures actually worked to end it by calling for a meeting of top officials. The date he gave for this meeting, December 12, 1997, was nearly four months after the violence erupted, by which time it had already subsided, and shortly before the elections took place. Ochieng, "Likoni: Sajjad....," *Daily Nation*.

1997.[282] The timing of the party's registration suggested that KANU permitted it to field candidates in order to ensure that if KANU was to lose the vote in Likoni district due to a voter backlash against the government that they had been unable to forestall, it at least was won by a KANU ally.[283] Since winning office, Shakombo has indeed aligned himself with KANU and cooperated with the ruling party.[284]

The Aftermath at the Coast: Failed Justice, Enduring Resentment

Failed Justice

The deeply flawed Kenyan justice system provided near total impunity for the 1997 Coast Province violence, as in other incidents of politically motivated ethnic attacks in Kenya before and since. Police investigations were seriously inadequate, and courts eventually acquitted all but a tiny handful of the accused raiders. The Akiwumi Commission, particularly in the first months of its existence, uncovered further evidence that had never been used in the criminal trials. Press accounts of testimony before the Akiwumi Commission generated hopes that the commission's work might serve as a springboard for addressing the long-standing impunity enjoyed by instigators of ethnic violence. To date, however, the government has refused to make public the commission's report and offers no indication that it intends to take seriously recommendations the commission was mandated to offer, nor has it used the information collected by the commission as the basis for

---

[282] In late 1997 the party was temporarily threatened with deregistration, but ultimately no action was taken. Maguta Kimemia, "Shirikisho Party 'not behind clashes,'" *Daily Nation*, July 30, 1998.

[283] KHRC has stated that the registration of the Shirikisho Party, by providing an outlet for the political expression of the indigenous population of the Coast following widespread police abuses, "helped reduce the antagonism toward Moi and his party, KANU." KHRC, *Kayas Revisited*, p. 46.

[284] Gitau Warigi, "Nyachae, Kanu and campaign hurdles ahead," *Daily Nation*, August 13, 2000. In 2001 President Moi suggested that SPK would merge with KANU, but party leaders rejected the plan, blaming Shakombo for devising it without their consent. "President Moi: Merger," *Daily Nation*, July 27, 2001; Patrick Beja, "Shirikisho says no to merger," *East African Standard*, July 29, 2001.

criminal prosecutions.[285] To deflect criticism for its inaction, the government announced in October 2000 that it had opened new investigations, but in light of past failings there was little hope these would lead to concrete results.

The raiders' accounts shed light on the matter of impunity. Of the five raiders interviewed by Human Rights Watch, two were never apprehended during the wave of arrests, one was quickly released together with a friend following the intervention of the prominent local businessman who had recruited him, one was released shortly after being jailed, and one was detained for a long period before being acquitted for lack of evidence. The raiders stated that all of their leaders, to their knowledge, escaped arrest. (As noted, several of them were killed in a police ambush a year and a half after the Likoni raid.)

The Police Investigation

The lack of seriousness in the government's investigative effort is most clearly demonstrated by the official police report on the Coast violence. The investigating officer who began to uncover important evidence was soon transferred, as noted above, and more junior personnel took over the investigation under the supervision of a PCIO and PPO who, having just arrived to replace transferred personnel, were new to the investigation. Although fifty-nine pages long, the police report contained only a very brief (ten pages) and superficial analysis, and offered no evidence to support its conclusions. The report largely blamed the violence on the National African Development Union (NADU), an unregistered Coast-based party, and its leader Ali Chizondo, whom it accused of organizing the raids. Two reasons were given: an official said he had been told that Chizondo recruited youth to fight the government because the party had been denied registration, and NADU's strong and public pro-majimbo stance (a stance which, the report did not mention, was shared by many KANU politicians). The police report also stated that local Muslim leaders incited the attacks, reportedly over a heated dispute about a local mosque, and accused several such leaders of supporting, and even participating, in the violence, but did not provide evidence for these claims. It named Alfan as the principal oath administrator for the raiders, again without specifying on what basis it reached this conclusion, even though police later testified they had an abundance of evidence. Strikingly, the report

---

[285] Human Rights Watch recognizes that not all information provided to the commission would be admissible in a criminal trial. The International Covenant on Civil and Political Rights (ICCPR) provides that a person cannot be "compelled to testify against himself or to confess guilt." ICCPR, Article 14(3)g, G.A. res. 2200A (XXI), 21 U.N. GAOR Supp. (No. 16) at 52, U.N. Doc. A/6316 (1966), entered into force Mar. 23, 1976.

noted that, besides NADU, no opposition parties had been implicated, while omitting any reference to the widely reported role of KANU officials other than noting that suspects named Shakombo, who was seeking the KANU nomination, as a key supporter and financier.[286]

The bulk of the police report consisted of more than forty pages of appendices. Among these were various lists that specified names of: those charged before the court (at that time, 169 of 545 men arrested); "recruited thugs" (381 people, divided into sub-groups or "squads"); "prime suspects," including Alfan, Chizondo, Maitha, and Masumbuko (only Chizondo was named in the main portion of the report); "thugs" killed in the security operation (twelve people); and suspects at large (twenty-two people). Again, however, the police did not indicate how they came to identify suspects, so this information was of little value, particularly for the purposes of criminal prosecution. For example, the report did not specify whether the list of suspected raiders was culled from the raiders' register or from other sources.

The Trials

Judges who oversaw the criminal cases of those charged in connection with the Likoni violence harshly criticized the police for making numerous, serious mistakes—a significant statement given the importance of the case. Among other criticisms, they said that police prosecutors failed to produce even circumstantial evidence linking the suspects to their alleged crimes, to explain the grounds for arrests, or to provide other required documentation. Instead, according to one judge, police offered only "gossip and rumor."[287]

Given the shoddy police investigation, the judges in the criminal cases said, they had no choice but to acquit the accused, some 240 people, all of whom had pleaded not guilty to charges of oath-taking, arson, theft, possession of offensive weapons, and robbery with violence. By the time these decisions were issued, from mid-1998 to early 1999, most of the accused had been in remand prison for more than a year, during which time several suspects had died. The long delay can partly be explained by the fact that prosecutors combined the cases against the 240 suspects, each charged with multiple crimes (many faced eighteen counts), and

---

[286] "Police Report-Likoni." Chizondo maintained he was innocent and claimed the government used him as a scapegoat. Human Rights Watch interview with Ali Said Chizondo, Tiwi, April 21, 1999.

[287] Francis Thoya, "17 Likoni suspects freed," *Daily Nation*, November 27, 1998; Francis Thoya, "Police criticised over Likoni trial," *Daily Nation*, December 23, 1998.

only separated the cases into smaller groupings and issued new charges (limited to six per person) on the orders of the High Court.[288]

While the suspected raiders were charged together (and later acquitted together), a few cases that went to trial separately resulted in convictions. In one, four suspects were sentenced to death for a September 1997 armed robbery reportedly carried out with a gun stolen from the Likoni police station. In another, a man who led police to a stolen gun was sentenced to four years in jail for weapons possession. In a third case, two juveniles and an adult were convicted on robbery charges and sentenced to death. These apparently were the only convictions for crimes that, according to prosecutors, were associated with the Likoni violence.[289]

The Akiwumi Commission: Dashed Hopes

The Akiwumi Commission was established in July 1998. Under its terms of reference, the duties of the Akiwumi Commission centered upon the investigation of the so-called "tribal clashes" (inter-ethnic violence) that occurred in Kenya between 1991 and 1998, in particular the causes of the violence, the actions of police and other law enforcement agencies in addressing these incidents, and the level of preparedness and efficacy of law enforcement agencies to prevent and control such violence. The commission was to recommend further investigation or prosecution of perpetrators of the incidents, as required, as well as ways to better prevent and control future inter-ethnic attacks.[290]

The commission, which sat for eleven months and overlapped with criminal proceedings related to the Likoni violence, heard a great deal of evidence linking ruling party politicians to the violence. Particularly during the time it sat in Mombasa, the commission very actively explored all evidence and subpoenaed politicians whose testimony it wished to hear. After the lead assisting counsel, who called witnesses and led much of the questioning, was replaced by the director of

---

[288] See, for example, "Four Likoni raid suspects died while in prison," *Daily Nation*, March 19, 1998; Thoya, "Police criticised...," *Daily Nation*; "Likoni suspects freed," *Daily Nation*, January 8, 1999; Francis Thoya, "Fresh charges for Likoni suspects," *Daily Nation*, February 11, 1998. A total of 702 people were arrested and interrogated by police and 350 of those were charged in connection with the Likoni violence, according to the government. Emman Omari, "88 Likoni raid victims identified," *Daily Nation*, April 22, 1998.

[289] Francis Thoya and Lilian Nduta, "Likoni: 4 sentences to death," *Daily Nation*, November 13, 1998; "Likoni suspects freed," *Daily Nation*; Francis Thoya, "It's death for 2 juveniles over Likoni killing," *Daily Nation*, July 24, 2001.

[290] Gazette Notice No. 3313: The Commissions of Inquiry Act, *Kenya Gazette* (Nairobi), July 1, 1998.

public prosecutions, Bernard Chunga (later named Chief Justice of Kenya), the commission focused less intently on the role of politicians. For example, they refused to hear testimony implicating politicians in the organization of the Rift Valley violence of the early 1990s, although lawyers representing the Law Society of Kenya played a key role, to the extent possible, in bringing forth evidence and focusing the commission's attention on indicators of state sponsorship of ethnic violence. Moreover, the presidentially appointed commission interpreted its regulations to the effect that any testimony that implicated President Moi himself would be admissible only on the basis of prior notification and approval by the commissioners; such testimony given without their permission would be expunged from the record.[291] This occurred on at least one occasion.[292] One witness refused to testify, declaring that the president, who himself had been implicated, had no "moral authority" to establish the commission or receive its report.[293] In addition, a problem arose in terms of the security of witnesses to the Akiwumi Commission, several of whom received threats.

In addition, the Akiwumi hearings uncovered extensive evidence of government laxity in its security response, as well as in the criminal trials of accused raiders. For example, police testimony to the commission revealed that key evidence was ignored in the criminal trials. The then-criminal investigations officer for Coast Province, who testified about key evidence recovered at the time of Swaleh bin Alfan's arrest, said that photographs and a notebook containing some of the raiders' records were shown to various other top officials, including the director of the Criminal Investigations Department in Nairobi and the Kenyan Police Commissioner. He said he was unaware why these were never presented as evidence in court.[294]

The Akiwumi Commission also brought to light the existence of the books recovered from the raiders' hideout, which contained names and other incriminating information. Police had not introduced this evidence in criminal court, and this omission is all the more striking given statements by police that they

---

[291] "Rules of practice bent to protect those mentioned from scrutiny," *People*, October 28, 2001. See also Gazette Notice No. 3477: The Judicial Commissions of Inquiry Act, Rules and Procedure, *Kenya Gazette*, July 10, 1998, regarding treatment of evidence on "any matter prejudicial to the security of the state or the Head of State."

[292] "Rules of practice...," *People*.

[293] Michael Njuguna and Watoro Kamau, "Mazrui must testify, commissioners say," *Daily Nation*, February 19, 1999.

[294] Akiwumi Commission Official Transcript, October 6, 1998, pp. 44-53; Mumo and Mayoyo, "Police boss...," *Daily Nation*; Mugasia, "Raid thought...," *East African Standard*.

used the information in the books to help them identify suspects who were subsequently arrested.[295] There also was much speculation at the Akiwumi hearings that pages identifying the raiders' financiers had been removed.[296] Such suspicions were aggravated by other indications of irregular record keeping and mishandling of the evidence.[297]

Evidence introduced at the Akiwumi hearings also pointed to an apparent police cover-up. It was revealed that the officer from Nairobi who was coordinating the Likoni investigations suggested that sworn statements attributed to Maitha and Masumbuko, which implicated the government in the organized political violence in Coast Province, be kept from the public. In an August 24, 1997, report to the Kenyan police commissioner, the investigating officer described police evidence linking Maitha and Masumbuko to the 1997 violence. He also included a comment, later read aloud before the Akiwumi Commission, drawing attention to:

> [Maitha and Masumbuko's] very complicated statements in which they revealed their previous activities in helping the Government in fighting political enemies [...]. [I]f their previous activities is [sic] anything to go by, then they are suspects prosecutable of [sic] conducting these activities. We find it quite implicating to use those statements in the open court because they are in bad taste and may not be good enough for the good name of our Government.[298]

The police commissioner testified that it was improper for the officer to have tried to hide these statements, as "there was nothing to hide," and said he had never

---

[295] See, for example, Amadi Mugasia, "Lawyer: Clashes rigging plot," *East African Standard*, September 25, 1998.

[296] Mugasia, "Lawyer: Clashes...," *East African Standard*; Mumo and Kithi, "Inquiry told of altered journals," *Daily Nation*.

[297] The DCIO testified that she was instructed to keep the books locked in a secure place and not to reveal their existence to the press, noting that they were never officially logged or presented in court. However, at the Akiwumi hearings, police produced an undated list of criminal court exhibits purporting to show that the books had been submitted as evidence in the trial, which a commission member and the police officer agreed appeared as if it had been added after the fact. Mugasia, "Lawyer: Clashes...," *East African Standard*; Mumo and Kithi, "Inquiry told of altered journals," *Daily Nation*.

[298] Akiwumi Commission Official Transcript, October 14, 1998, pp. 76-78.

seen the statements until they were made public at the Akiwumi Commission.[299] Masumbuko's statement, it was confirmed, was never introduced in his criminal trial, and use of the statement attributed to Maitha was blocked by judicial order.[300]

The difference in approach between the deeply flawed criminal trials and the Akiwumi Commission, which led to far more useful revelations about the Likoni violence, raised hopes that the commission's final report to the president would include important recommendations for the prosecution of the main figures behind that violence and in that way finally break the long cycle of impunity over politically motivated ethnic violence in Kenya. The acquittal of the 240 suspects who were tried in connection with the Likoni violence cast serious doubt on the ability of the proceedings of the Akiwumi Commission to be of assistance in obtaining any redress for the victims.[301]

The Akiwumi Commission submitted its much anticipated final report to the president in August 1999. In December of that year, responding to repeated queries from members of parliament, a minister in the Office of the President said that the government was still reviewing the report.[302] He added that recommendations made by the commission relating to prosecution of those implicated required further investigation and stated that some of the other recommendations would be implemented before the report was made public. In October 2000, again in response to a public query, Kenya's attorney-general announced that, in keeping with a recommendation of the commission, police had just begun new investigations into the Likoni violence, were taking statements from suspects and witnesses, and would initiate prosecutions against the perpetrators once sufficient evidence had been gathered.[303]

---

[299] Akiwumi Commission Official Transcript, June 4, 1999, p. 110-111.

[300] Akiwumi Commission Official Transcript, June 4, 1999, pp. 111-112; Francis Thoya, "MP fearing, court told," *Daily Nation*, December 12, 1998.

[301] See, for example, Matikio Bohoko, "Commentary: Moi may recall Akiwumi Commission of inquiry," *Concord* (Mombasa), September 22-29, 1998; Thoya, "Police criticised...," *Daily Nation*. Any effort to bring new cases in connection with the Likoni violence might be subject to the prohibition against double jeopardy, or prosecution twice for the same crime. ICCPR, Article 14(7), G.A. res. 2200A (XXI), 21 U.N. GAOR Supp. (No. 16) at 52, U.N. Doc. A/6316 (1966), entered into force Mar. 23, 1976.

[302] "Clashes report 'being studied,'" *Daily Nation*, December 9, 1999.

[303] "Clashes Report Calls for Inquiries," *Daily Nation*, October 5, 2000. The provincial police officer for Coast Province had confirmed a day earlier that an investigation had been initiated, but said he did not have any further details. Willis Oketch, "Police launch fresh investigations into clashes," *East African Standard*, October 4, 2000.

The government, however, has not taken seriously its responsibility to promptly, thoroughly, and impartially investigate ethnic violence and to bring those responsible to justice. The announcement of new police investigations came nearly a year after the government first had said such investigations would be launched. Well over a year after that, there was still no news of progress in the police investigations and it was not clear that such an investigation was underway. Moreover—despite a public clamor for the report and lawsuits filed to compel its release—more than two and one-half years after its submission, the government had yet to make public the commission's report.[304] Nor had it made arrests or initiated prosecutions of those believed to be responsible for instigating ethnic violence elsewhere in the country. Frustrated at the persistent impunity, in mid-2001 victims of the Likoni violence indicated that they planned to sue the government for damages, as did victims of ethnic violence elsewhere in the country.[305]

Enduring Resentment

The raiders interviewed by Human Rights Watch felt they had been used by politicians for their own ends. They had agreed to use violent means to oust up-country residents and obtain land, they said, to secure majimbo. It was clear they did not act because they had an interest in ensuring a KANU victory at the polls.

One raider was particularly outspoken about this, indicating that he felt KANU forced them to stop short of their goal in order to win the election: "[After the elections,] the politicians disassociated themselves from us [...] because they had their votes."[306] He explained:

> We were planning to do this thing ourselves and Swaleh had an idea with the politicians and they took advantage. The president for the election used us to disrupt and disperse people. [...Then,] once we'd flushed out the up-country people, they came to cool us down and fulfill the promises to take us abroad [for protection from arrest] or give us jobs. We saw Swaleh campaign for

---

[304] See, for example, Francis Thoya, "Lawyers demand Akiwumi report," *Daily Nation*, February 21, 2000; Francis Thoya, "Farmer Sues Over Akiwumi Report," *Daily Nation*, October 29, 2000.

[305] "Victims of political clashes demand government compensation," AFP, July 27, 2001; "Clash victims plan suit against State," *Daily Nation*, August 2, 2001.

[306] Human Rights Watch interview with Raider B, Ukunda, May 8, 1999.

KANU. At first, when we were organizing for the raids, he
mentioned nothing about elections. [...] Later I learned that
senior people wanted to chase up-country people so they
couldn't vote. I don't know if Swaleh had all the information or
if he was being used. We believe he's a big magician so we
have to be in good relations with him. Most of us are angry with
him. We never got what was promised.[307]

One raider stated: "We were promised we'd be given houses belonging to
up-country people and employment. We never got what was promised."[308]
Moreover, the raiders were distressed and extremely angry over the harsh and
indiscriminant reprisals by government forces against their community. They also
expressed rage and fear over the torture some of them had endured and made clear
that their anger against the authorities had deepened.

In general, the raiders were sorely disappointed that they did not succeed in
achieving majimbo. The poor conditions faced by the Digo community on the
South Coast remain unchanged. Shakombo testified that in his long experience as
a local leader he was convinced that the Digos, particularly those who had fought
in 1997, would not give up their dreams of majimbo. His February 1998 police
statement read: "Their believe [sic] is that, only [the] majimbo system can solve
their problem. I have heard through rumour that, oathing within [the] coast has
never stopped even after the clashes as the locals [sic] desire for majimboism have
[sic] not been attained. Nevertheless, I have no proof that the oathing is actually
taking place."[309]

---

[307] Human Rights Watch interview with Raider B, Mombasa, May 26, 1999. Alfan,
as noted above, also apparently felt he had been double-crossed by Coast Province KANU
leaders, whom he said had promised to reward him for his campaign activities.

[308] Human Rights Watch interview with Raider A, Ukunda, April 22, 1999.

[309] Kaona and Githua, "Shakombo says...," *East African Standard*; Statement Under
Inquiry dated February 28, 1998, copy on file with Human Rights Watch.

VI. OUTLOOK FOR THE FUTURE

A Time of Transition

Political debate in Kenya is once again heating up in the run-up to general elections set for 2002. Presidential succession has become the subject of much discussion and political intrigue. The jockeying for position has been particularly intense within the ruling party. President Moi has stated that he plans to step down as president and that the time has come for younger leaders to emerge.

In a move that has bolstered the ruling party's prospects for electoral success, in March 2002 KANU merged with the National Development Party (NDP), which has a largely Luo constituency. Moi, who had arranged the merger, was elected to the newly created and powerful post of chair of the merged party, which at this writing retained the name KANU. Moi also sought to broaden the ethnic base of the ruling party by recruiting politicians from communities associated with the opposition—including the Kikuyu—to join his government and giving them positions of prominence. Some in KANU and NDP had opposed the merger, but at this writing it remained unclear whether there would be significant defections to other parties. Five of Kenya's opposition parties, for their part, announced in February 2002 that they had joined forces and would work together to nominate candidates and, if elected, share power. The parliament's defeat of an anti-corruption bill personally endorsed by President Moi in August 2001 signaled the potential electoral strength of a united opposition.

Constitutional reform also has remained a topic of considerable debate, and the debate promised to grow in urgency with the approach of the 2002 national election. In January 2001 the chair of the government-appointed constitutional review commission was sworn in, and five months later the Moi government dropped its objections to the inclusion of civil society representatives in the commission. The commission announced in March 2002 that it would not be able to complete its work in advance of the presidential election.

In 2001 a top committee of the ruling party, joined by NDP, announced provisionally that the merged party would propose a major devolution of power to Kenya's regions under a federalism or majimbo model. Similarly, some politicians from other parties have also advanced majimbo proposals, drawing on the popularity of the concept in some parts of the country while generally seeking to distance themselves from the record of past ethnic violence in the name of majimbo. At times the new calls for majimbo have echoed those of the past, raising the specter of ethnic expulsions and violence. For example, a prominent KANU politician was quoted as stating in September 2001 that unless majimbo was introduced, Kenya would face "more bloodshed than that witnessed in Israel and

Palestine today."[310] Some figures in the opposition have promoted the idea of a transitional government or government of national unity to oversee the implementation of a new constitutional framework and to help ensure the fairness of the national election. There have also been calls for early elections from some quarters.

Kenya, facing an important presidential election and the outcome of the critical constitutional reform process, is at a political crossroads. President Moi's commitment to step down from power, together with his efforts to build a broader ethnic coalition in support of the ruling party and the expectation that he will designate his intended successor, have led some to anticipate that the political transition in Kenya to a post-Moi regime will be relatively smooth. At the same time, deadly inter-ethnic attacks in late 2001 and early 2002 attested to the potential for outbreaks of violence in the run-up to the 2002 elections, particularly when political leaders inflame ethnic tensions. Corruption, insecurity, and the sorry state of Kenya's judicial system were among the problems that continued to corrode public faith in the government. Moreover, the lack of accountability for past politically motivated attacks has contributed to very specific fears by victimized communities that they could once again become targets for electoral violence.

Guns at the Ready

Rising insecurity in Kenya, particularly the increased availability of small arms, has made more volatile an already precarious situation. The proliferation of automatic weapons among many pastoralist groups in northern Kenya in particular raises the possibility of an escalation into clan warfare. This is especially true in northwest Kenya. In the North Rift Valley, tensions between pastoralist communities over armed cattle rustling incidents and loss of life have repeatedly erupted into large-scale violence, with no effective government intervention.

For a recent example, in March 2001 more than fifty people from the Marakwet clan were killed by Pokot cattle raiders who burned hundreds of structures and stole thousands of livestock. Local leaders accused the government of laxity in its response, saying it failed to respond to a warning of an attack. One leader stated: "The government machinery has been quick to deal ruthlessly and mercilessly with the Marakwet whenever they are on a revenge mission in Pokot but will turn a blind eye or look unable to do the same when Pokots raid Marakwet

---

[310] "Kenya: Minister launches newspaper to campaign for federalism," *East African Standard*, BBC Monitoring, September 9, 2001. The speaker stated that he was not advocating the expulsion of non-indigenous residents: "We all love one another and *majimbo* will ensure the continuity of this." Ibid.

in broad daylight."[311] An unconfirmed estimate suggests that, between them, the Pokot and Marakwet communities have at least 9,000 small arms and perhaps as many as 20,000, while conservative figures from confidential government security reports are said to indicate that there are at least 4,000 firearms, including G3 rifles and AK-47s, in civilian hands in Pokot, Turkana, and Marakwet districts in the North Rift area.[312]

The Kenyan foreign minister was reported to have suggested in early 2001 that the way to respond to the situation in the North Rift was to disarm the communities and leave security in the hands of the security organs and police reservists.[313] This was unlikely to have reassured the Marakwet, since the government is often accused of selectively arming Pokots under the police reservist program, and it has long been alleged that Pokots use the government-issued weapons to carry out cattle raids throughout the North Rift.[314] One leader stated:

> We know that Kenyatta [Moi's predecessor] armed Pokot to act as a buffer zone from external raiders emanating from neighboring countries. However, the community have turned the same guns against their immediate neighbours, with the Marakwet and Turkana suffering most.[315]

High tensions between pastoralists in northwest Kenya have been further aggravated by politicians who advance a divisive ethic agenda. Francis Lotodo, who served in the Moi cabinet from 1998 until his death in November 2000 and was considered a close ally to President Moi, was notorious for making inflammatory statements.[316] For example, in 1999 he reportedly told all Marakwets

---

[311] "Anger mounts over Pokot killings," *Daily Nation*, March 14, 2001.

[312] Judith Achieng, "Government accused of laxity in probing cattle thefts," IPS, March 26, 2001; Muggah and Berman, *Humanitarianism Under Threat*, p. 66.

[313] "Minister says deal on small arms imminent" *Daily Nation*, March 26, 2001.

[314] KHRC, *Raiding Democracy: the Slaughter of the Marakwet in Kerio Valley*, (Nairobi: Kenya Human Rights Commission, 2001), pp. 41-43.

[315] "Anger Mounts...," *Daily Nation*.

[316] He was reportedly charged with incitement in 1997 for "making war-like statements" (the charge was dropped), had earlier been charged and jailed for "promoting war-like activities" in 1984, and was temporarily expelled from KANU in 1989. "Kenya's energy minister dies in South African hospital," Associated Press, November 9, 2000; Kaplish Barsito, "Why the Pokots weep as they bury the king," *Daily Nation*, November 18, 2000.

living in West Pokot District that they should "pack and move out" before the year's end and instructed Pokot youths to make sure that the "Marakwet is not given room in the Pokot land."[317] The use of inflammatory rhetoric in the North Rift did not end with Lotodo's death; to the contrary, incitement by Pokot leaders reportedly increased in 2001.[318]

The arming of Pokot men, combined with inflammatory comments by politicians, the absence of accountability for such statements, and the lackluster response of security forces to Pokot raids, have contributed to open speculation that the government at some level may have a hand in spurring the violence. Some leaders of other pastoralist communities in the North Rift Valley have accused the government of at least tacitly, if not openly, supporting the Pokot raids, even referring in one case to "a government-sponsored Pokot invasion."[319]

The situation in the North Rift remains explosive. The deputy secretary-general of the National Council of Churches of Kenya blamed insecurity on both the "influx of small arms" from neighboring countries and "careless utterances and incitement" by politicians representing the Pokot, Marakwet, and Turkana communities in the North Rift.[320] The Kenya Human Rights Commission has argued similarly that the deadly raids in northern Kenya, particularly those carried out by the Pokot community that has received arms from the government, are part of a strategy by the ruling party to use intimidation tactics to reestablish political dominance in parts of Rift Valley Province in advance of the 2002 elections.[321] A December 2001 NCCK report on violence in the North Rift likewise pointed to the dangerous linkages between arms and political incitement and attributed much of the violence in the North Rift to the combination of both factors.[322] Unfortunately, the Kenyan government has thus far failed to take action to counteract this crucial nexus between arms availability and divisive political agendas.

---

[317] "Lotodo censures KenGen over jobs," *Daily Nation*, November 11, 1999. Lotodo was reported to have made similar remarks later in 1999, which he denied. "Minister denies telling non-Pokots to leave," *Daily Nation*, December 31, 1999.

[318] KHRC, *Raiding Democracy,* pp. 48-52.

[319] "Editorial: When will govt act in the North Rift?" *Daily Nation*, March 11, 2000. See also, David Mugonyi, "Ex-MP says Govt abetting rustling," *Daily Nation*, March 13, 2000; Gitau Warigi, "Who's Fuelling Cattle Rustling by the Pokot?" *East African Standard*, February 14, 2000.

[320] "Probe arms influx, cleric urges state," *Daily Nation*, April 15, 2001.

[321] KHRC, *Raiding Democracy*, pp. 3, 24-29, 37-45.

[322] Ken Ramani, "The guns of Kerio Valley and the looming danger," *East African Standard*, December 11, 2001.

There are other potential flashpoints for politically charged inter-ethnic violence in Kenya, as evidenced by violence in late 2001 and early 2002 that together took dozens of lives. In December 2001, following a visit to the area by President Moi, a rent dispute in the Kibera slum of Nairobi erupted into violence by attackers armed with clubs and machetes, resulting in more than a dozen deaths. Members of the political opposition, as well as some civic leaders and landlords, blamed President Moi and a minister in his government, who they alleged incited the violence with comments favoring the tenants.[323] In Tana River district, in the interior of Coast Province, 2001 saw repeated incidents of violence, particularly late in the year, that resulted in over one hundred deaths. Again, politicians were accused of fanning the flames of ethnic tensions. In this case, religious leaders, opposition politicians, and President Moi himself attributed the violence at least in part to inflammatory statements by politicians.[324] Allegations of incitement to violence also surfaced in connection with the brutal slaying of more than twenty people in March 2002 in the Kariobangi North slum of Nairobi, which were attributed to a youth gang.[325]

Elsewhere in the country, some groups have organized themselves into militias, ostensibly to be able to defend their communities against attack. In other cases, a group's mistrust of the Moi government and fear of being targeted for political violence has been the prime motivation for secretly organizing and acquiring arms. A 1998 government report found that victims of ethnic violence in Rift Valley Province "were prepared (or indeed were preparing) to organise their own security."[326]

---

[323] "Minister accused of instigating clashes in Nairobi slum district," KTN TV in BBC Monitoring, December 4, 2001; Marc Lacey, "Residents Flee Slum in Nairobi After 12 Are Killed in Clashes" *New York Times*, December 6, 2001; "Kenya's slum war," BBC, December 7, 2001; "Slum women march to Moi's office," *Daily Nation*, December 7, 2001; Marc Lacey, "Officials Gather in Nairobi Slum To Quell Deadly Rent Clashes," *New York Times*, December 9, 2001.

[324] "Opposition party official arrested over ethnic violence in southeast," KTN TV in BBC Monitoring, December 16, 2001; "Religious leaders blame government over ethnic clashes," *Daily Nation*, December 9, 2001; "President Moi visits slum area affected by clashes" KBC radio, December 7, 2001; "Police reservists disarmed in Tana River," IRIN, January 4, 2002.

[325] David Mageria, "Kenyans warn of tribal conflict after slum carnage," Reuters, March 7, 2002.

[326] Standing Committee on Human Rights (Kenya), *First Public Report of the Standing Committee on Human Rights* (Nairobi: December 1998), p. 143.

Members of the Kikuyu, Kenya's largest ethnic group and a frequent target of state-sponsored attacks, confirmed in 1999 that they were very conscious of their security and had taken steps they hoped would defend them from any renewed violence. In some communities, they said, Kikuyus have procured some weapons and organized small armed groups to protect themselves in anticipation of renewed violence. For example, a Kikuyu elder stated that Kikuyus in central Kenya, whom he described as relatively well-off and strong in number, were better prepared for violence than their fellow Kikuyus in other parts of the country. But he added that elsewhere Kikuyus were beginning to take similar steps:

> The idea of organizing people to arm themselves came to us this year [in 1999]. We have seen the symptoms...Everyone in this country is feeling insecure unless you are KAMATUSA [an acronym used to describe the ethnic groups most closely associated with KANU]...Kalenjins are well-armed; now the Kikyus, Kisii, and Luhya are preparing to defend themselves."[327]

When violence broke out in Rift Valley Province's Laikipia district in early 2000 for the second time in as many years, opposition politicians reportedly proclaimed that the people of Laikipia should be armed and that they were willing to contribute the funds necessary to purchase the weapons.[328] The following year an MP representing Laikipia stated:

> It should be noted that all the neighbors of the Kikuyu in Laikipia—the Maasai, Samburu, Tugen and Pokot—have guns and homeguards [referring to police reservists]. The government has left only the Kikuyu without guns.... I am calling on the Minister in charge of Internal Security to end insecurity in Laikipia. So far, I have been pleading with the Kikuyu to restrain themselves. I am not ready to sacrifice my political career by trying to avert tribal clashes, which is a Government responsibility. [The government should defend the Kikuyu] or we shall use every way possible to defend ourselves.[329]

---

[327] Human Rights Watch interview with a Kikuyu elder, Nakuru, Kenya, May 14, 1999.

[328] "Kenya: Opposition MPs claim killings in central region 'state-sponsored,'"*East African Standard*, BBC Monitoring, January 24, 2000.

[329] Muthui Mwai, "Stop these raids, MP tells State," *Daily Nation*, April 7, 2001.

The vicious cycle of self-arming raises the risk that armed confrontations might be sparked and, in a politically charged environment, quickly spread. So long as the Kenyan government neglects to take measures to control weapons flows, to ensure that politicians are not able to arm groups, and to guarantee accountability for past political violence, the potential for renewed violence and accompanying human rights abuse persists. Political disputes risk turning violent, ethnic tensions risk being manipulated or sparking bloodshed independently, and marginalized populations risk taking weapons into their own hands. Kenyans have on the whole resisted turning to armed violence to settle grievances, but the risks are too high and the past too instructive for that possibility to be ignored.

VII. KENYA AND THE INTERNATIONAL COMMUNITY

President Moi has benefited enormously from his position as the longtime leader of a country that is considered a linchpin of stability in a region marked by a great deal of turmoil. This leverage has translated into perpetual forgiveness for the government's behavior by diplomats, even when at a high cost to human rights. In part, Moi has remained a reliable, if often difficult, ally to Western governments over the years because no clear political alternative has emerged. Foreign governments have certainly expressed dissatisfaction with aspects of Moi's rule and condemned politically motivated violence, but they have not made it a priority to press him to rein in KANU politicians and government allies whose rhetoric and actions clearly undermine public security. Moi has done the minimum necessary to deflect criticism of his government's record on this point: create commissions or committees whose work never results in action, much less accountability.

President Moi has been able to ignore important dimensions of the security problems facing Kenya because he has skillfully focused rhetoric and (sometimes) action on the areas of most immediate concern to the international donors on whom the country depends. Corruption is a primary issue in this regard and continues to receive much high-level attention. Security issues have taken on increasing importance, however, since the 1998 bombing of the U.S. embassy in Nairobi, and the September 11, 2001, attacks in the United States. But security concerns have been narrowly defined.

In recent years the Moi government has focused on major security threats in the region, and more recently the related problem of weapons inflows, but this approach has not been comprehensive nor rights-based. To the contrary, it has looked almost exclusively at the movement of weapons into Kenya from neighboring countries. To a degree, it also has focused on the channels that permit the illegal sale of these weapons inside the country. For this crackdown, it has largely targeted refugees living in Kenya, particularly Somalis, whom it blames wholesale for the problem of weapons proliferation. The government's actions, purportedly directed to stop crime, have undermined refugee protections against vulnerable groups. International donors have been loath to criticize such behavior.

Moreover, the Kenyan government, its partners in regional small arms control initiatives, and its backers in the international community have highlighted concerns about crime and rising insecurity in the country, but they have thus far disregarded the risk that firearms may be used to carry out politically motivated attacks. The 1997 Coast Province violence revealed how well-organized attackers mobilized around a clear political agenda and with relatively few guns could terrorize an area for weeks and leave a legacy of human devastation, physical destruction, bitterness, economic decline, and ethnic animosity. A solution to this

114

complex problem demands attention to the root causes of such discontent, but also to the irresponsible political discourse that stokes ethnic tensions and the formation by politicians of organized groups that carry out acts of violence on their behalf. So long as politicians are not held to account for inciting violence and are instead able to mobilize armed groups to carry out the dirty work, violence will continue to be used as a political tool. Add to that the ability to obtain weapons, whether stolen or purchased, and Kenya faces a much more explosive problem.

VIII. CONCLUSION

Past politically motivated ethnic violence in Kenya, which has flared especially at election time, raises serious concerns that politicians may orchestrate violence to influence the next general elections, slated for 2002. This concern is rooted in several factors. Electoral politics in Kenya are split along ethnic lines, pitting ethnic groups against each other in a competition for power and resources. Kenya's history of politically motivated violence targeting particular groups clearly suggest tactics political opportunists can emulate to achieve similar results, which they are all the more likely to pursue since the masterminds of past attacks have enjoyed impunity for their actions. Violence has been used so often for political ends and without accountability that it is at risk of being seen as a legitimate means of political discourse. The reliance on violence and the targeting of victims along ethnic lines, when combined with the increased availability of small arms, makes for an ever more dangerous mix. Those who have been the targets of past attacks have resented the suffering of their community and have reacted to fears about the future by increasingly seeking self-protection through the acquisition of more sophisticated weapons. This growing militarization and fear of other groups raises the possibility that ethnic violence in Kenya might be triggered easily and spread rapidly, with devastating results.

IX. FULL RECOMMENDATIONS

To the Government of Kenya

With Respect to Political Violence and Human Rights:

- Take action to prevent politically motivated violence and ensure accountability for past incidents of such violence, including incidents carried out with state sponsorship. Make public in full the findings and recommendations of the government's commission of inquiry into ethnic violence (the Akiwumi Commission); bring the perpetrators to justice, regardless of their political affiliation; and renounce violence by the ruling party.

- Pay reparations to the victims of state-sponsored violence.

With Respect to Security Issues:

- Strengthen legal controls on firearms and ammunition. Revise legislation to ensure that it reflects the highest standard and is comprehensive. This should encompass the manufacture, possession, and transfer of these weapons—inclusive of export, import, sale, transshipment, and transport—both within Kenya and with respect to international transactions. Strictly enforce these legal controls, including by: ensuring that security forces are adequately trained and equipped; enhancing the capacity of customs officials to identify and inspect suspicious cargo; combating corruption among law enforcement personnel; and ensuring accountability for misconduct.

- Improve national controls over weapons stocks. Specifically: ensure strict stockpile management and storage of government-held weapons and ammunition to prevent their loss, theft, or illegal sale; responsibly dispose of (for example, through destruction) all seized, surrendered, and surplus weapons to prevent their further diffusion and misuse; require all legally held firearms to be registered, together with ammunition, and closely monitor the use of these weapons.

- Continue to engage with regional partners to harmonize legal controls and improve law enforcement cooperation, with a focus on concrete results.

Adopt the proposed regional legal protocol and implement it into national legislation.

*   Enhance transparency. Prepare and make public on an annual basis a detailed national report on the manufacture, transfer (inclusive of export, import, sale, transshipment, and transport), and accumulation of arms and ammunition. As part of this report, enhance transparency about the Eldoret ammunition factory, including with respect to production levels, volume of sale, and destination of ammunition sold. Report fully to the United Nations Register of Conventional Arms.

*   Strictly control arms transfers. Explicitly define national criteria for authorizing arms transfers (again, inclusive of all categories, including transshipment). Develop and incorporate into law a code of conduct that strictly limits the transfer of weapons from or through Kenya, at a minimum to ensure that weapons transfers are not authorized to human rights abusers, countries that have inadequate controls on weapons, and areas (particularly neighboring countries) from which they might be diverted for re-sale inside Kenya. Incorporate into national legislation and strictly enforce United Nations sanctions prohibiting arms transfers to embargoed destinations, as well as nonbinding subregional, regional, and international measures circumscribing weapons transfers.

*   Ensure accountability of local security structures. Apply strict norms of discipline and accountability to the police reservist program or disband it. Bar the formation of community militias. Do not permit local communities to take on or share in law enforcement functions without strict oversight, proper training, full adherence to legal standards that are consistent with human rights norms, and accountability.

To the Governments of East Africa

*   Adopt a comprehensive approach to combat illicit weapons trafficking and, more generally, small arms proliferation in the region. With respect to legal controls, develop and adopt model legislation and, drawing on best practices and existing international commitments with regard to international arms transfers, devise and implement a subregional code of conduct. Adopt the code of conduct nationally, giving it legal status. With respect to transparency, enhance information-sharing and the public

dissemination of arms-related information, including by preparing and making public a subregional or regional arms register. With respect to law enforcement measures, as planned under a regional action plan, coordinate efforts through information exchanges; engage in joint operations; adopt a common marking and tracing system; harmonize customs controls; and cooperate to improve border controls. With respect to the demand for small arms: develop regional strategies (supplemented by national initiatives) to improve governance, alleviate poverty, and enhance security. With respect to the political dimension of armed violence, cease to arm members of unaccountable local security structures.

- Adopt changes at the national level to combat weapons proliferation and improve security, as above.

To International Donors and the International Community

- Work with the Kenyan government and other regional actors to enhance security and reform the security sector, to address the demand for weapons and the culture of violence, and to encourage progress with respect to small arms controls. Ensure that in all cases, human rights (inclusive of refugee rights) are not compromised.

- Support and expand support for community-based approaches to stem the demand for weapons, prevent crime, and reduce conflict among communities. Comprehensive community-based strategies might include various elements such as disarmament, public education, and use of conflict resolution techniques.

- Insist on governmental accountability for past incidents of ethnic and political violence involving agents of the state at any level. Press for needed reforms, as above, to prevent further such violence.

- Exercise restraint with respect to arms transfers to East Africa and the Great Lakes region, as well as other areas of violent conflict and countries where the diffusion of weapons could generate or contribute to a potentially excessive and destabilizing accumulation of weapons and thereby put human rights in danger.